THE WORLD'S GREATEST CRIMES

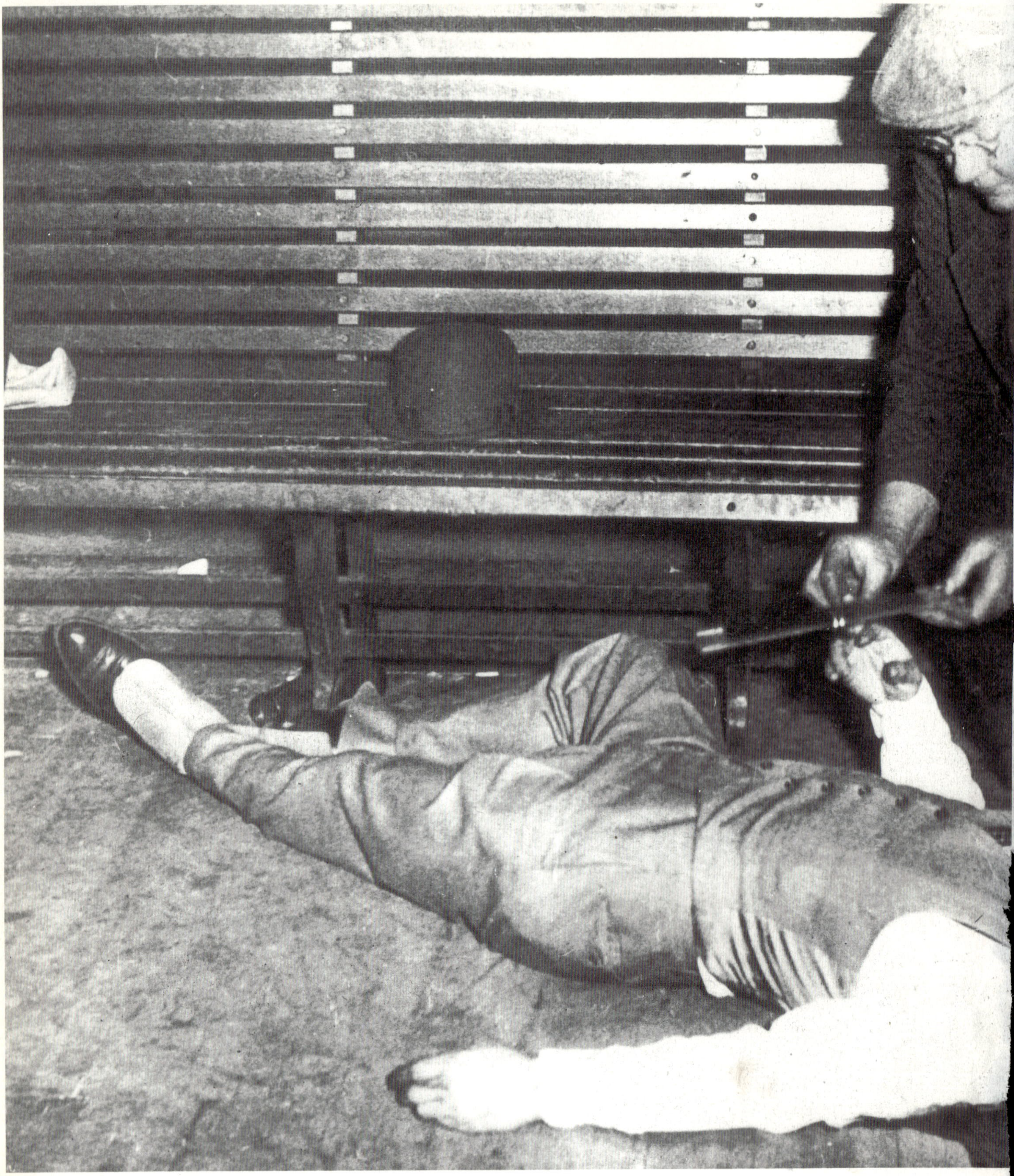

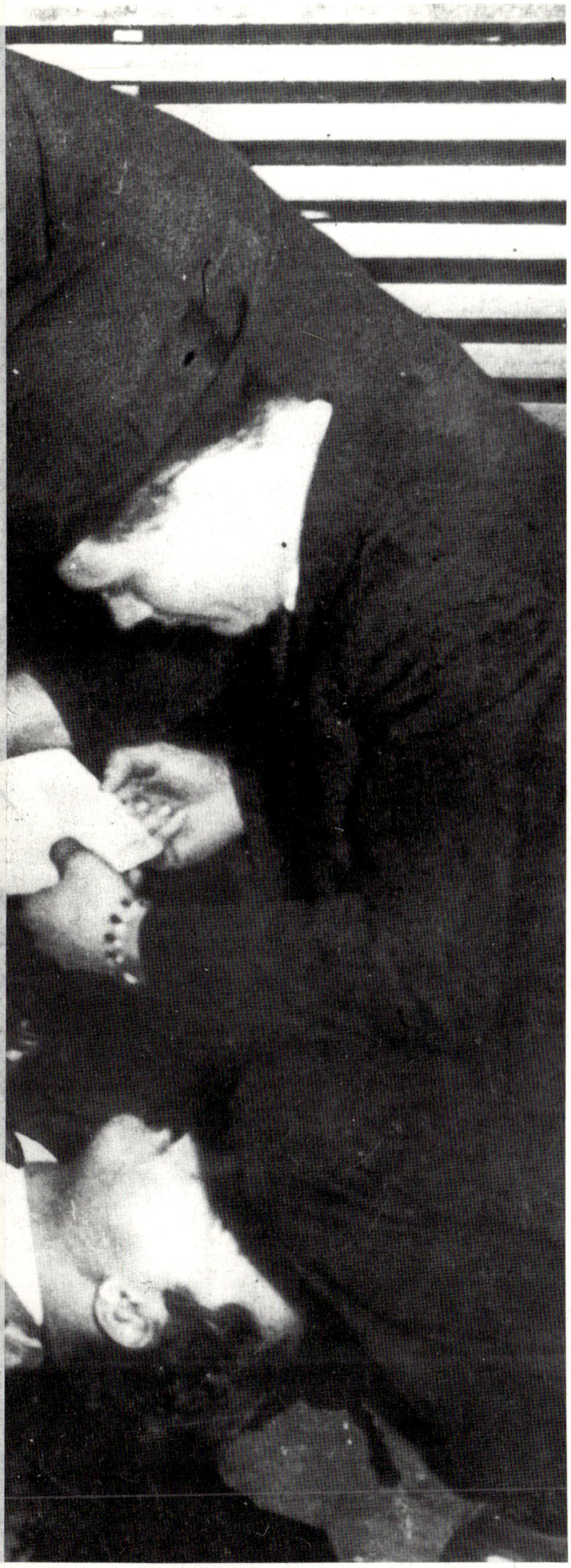

THE WORLD'S GREATEST CRIMES

Murder, Robbery and Mayhem
from 1900 to the Present Day

W. BARRINGTON KEITH

HAMLYN

Half-title page
Henri Landru in court.

Title page
The body of Jack McGurn, a henchman of Al Capone.

This page
The aftermath of the Great Train Robbery.

First published in 1990 by
The Hamlyn Publishing Group Limited
Michelin House, 81 Fulham Road,
London, SW3 6RB

ISBN 0 600 56810 5

Typeset by MS Filmsetting Limited, Frome, Somerset

Produced by Mandarin Offset
Printed and bound in Hong Kong

CONTENTS

INTRODUCTION

Perhaps the greatest crime of the century is being committed by the human race in general and involves the ultimate destruction of the planet by the abuse of its ecology. Perhaps the greatest crime, in a more conventional sense, is what is known as the Holocaust. Since neither of these topics is mentioned here, it might be as well to define the scope of the book.

With such a vast array of crime to choose from, the author and publishers have decided to ignore crimes by political organizations, crimes against the state, terrorism and espionage. They have decided to limit themselves to what might be called 'personal' or 'private' crimes, i.e. those in which the personalities and motives of an individual give the crime some appeal: in other words crimes in which the perpetrator makes some personal gain, like the removal of a rival, the satisfaction of some craving or the acquisition of money.

Two political assassinations are included, those of John F. Kennedy and Martin Luther King, because there is a continued interest in whether or not all the facts about them have come to light. Similarly, the killing of John Lennon is included because the personalities of Lennon and his killer are of interest. Otherwise the crimes are 'private' ones, those in which the fame or notoriety of the criminal or victim depend on the crime alone.

So far as 'private' crime is concerned, what constitutes a 'great' crime? Not, in the case of murder, the number of bodies. The fact that Charles Whitman killed 21 and wounded 28 in a morning by taking his collection of guns to the top of the observation tower at the University of Texas and using it as a sniping post, does not make his a 'great' crime, especially when it is known that the probable cause of his behaviour was a brain tumour. Similarly when it is stated that in 1955 Jack Graham took out insurance on his mother's life and then planted a bomb on the plane she caught from Denver, thus killing her and 43 other victims, there is not much else left to say.

We have chosen our 'great' crimes, therefore, on the basis of the degree of interest they provoked at the time they were committed, in the hope that some of that interest will be rekindled in the reader. Even so, a considerable amount of selection has had to be carried out. We have not included such mass killers as Wayne Williams, Ted Bundy or Paul Knowles since the careers of other mass murderers, such as the Yorkshire Ripper, the Son of Sam or the Vampire of Düsseldorf, which are included, seem more interesting. The story of Dean Corll, the homosexual killer who collected the bodies of boys in his boat shed is not included, since it is too similar to that of John Gacy, who kept the bodies under his house.

Some of the murderers whose stories are related here killed only once, but they provoked tremendous interest, such as the lovers Thompson and Bywaters in England, who disposed of an inconvenient husband, or the more sinister pair, Snyder and Gray, in America, who did the same but in very different circumstances.

It remains to be said that one or two 'crimes' included are not in one sense crimes at all, in that nobody was convicted of them. Thus the 'Dingo Baby' case of Australia was one in which the mother of the baby was accused of murder, but as she was eventually found not guilty there was no crime – unless a dingo can be called a criminal. And we have included the 'Mormon Sex in Chains' case which so titillated the British public in the 1960s, although in the end no one was brought to trial, the accused having fled the country. The only justification is that it is a good story – and we hope that you enjoy reading it, together with the others.

Left
Hawley Crippen, under arrest, is escorted ashore at Liverpool.

Centre left
Edith Thompson and Frederick Bywaters.

Centre right
John Wayne Gacy in his clown costume.

Bottom left
David Berkowitz between two police officers.

Bottom right
Peter Sutcliffe, covered by a blanket, being taken into a police station.

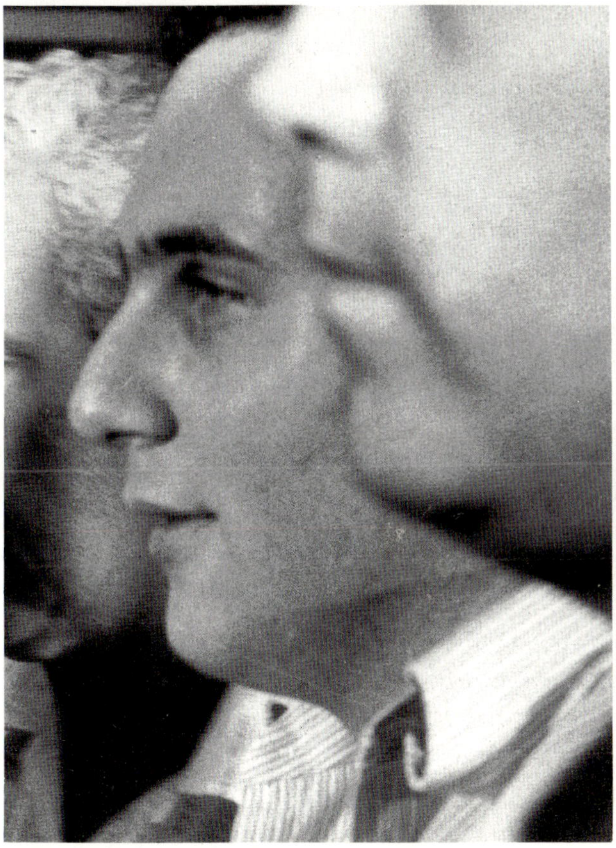

The First Two Decades

A velvet swing,
a mild-mannered murderer,
bridal baths and
a missing masterpiece.

Crowds gather outside the Old Bailey, London, in July 1915 at the end of the trial of George Joseph Smith.

THE CHORUS GIRL AND THE ARCHITECT

Mamzelle Champagne ***was a poor musical, but the society audience saw a drama of real-life tragedy too.***

'Tell me, pretty maiden, are there any more at home like you?' Evelyn Nesbit, to whom this song was sung when she was in the chorus of the musical *Floradora*, could justifiably answer that there were only a few, kind sir, in the whole world. For she had a remarkable, fragile beauty. Later, in court, giving evidence on behalf of the man who had killed for her honour, she was described as like a lily, and her beauty as 'something that lies over her face like a gossamer veil, infinitely appealing'.

If she was well-known for her looks, the man who was killed on her account, Stanford White, was famous for his skills. An architect, he was influential in giving New York the shape in which it moved into the 20th century. One of his creations became a landmark as New York's main arena for circuses, spectaculars and boxing matches, and it was the scene of his sensational murder in 1906: Madison Square Garden.

White was a big man with a flourishing moustache and, having made a fortune, he enjoyed spending it, mainly on parties for friends in artistic circles. The chorus line was where he looked for pretty girls to satisfy his sexual tastes, and soon after the turn of the century he met Evelyn Nesbit. She was an innocent, fresh beauty of 16; he was a man of the world, a seductive charmer of 47.

Evelyn was taken for lunch to his apartment on West 24th Street by a girlfriend, and afterwards White conducted them upstairs to a room where they played on a red velvet swing. Suspended from the ceiling was a large Japanese umbrella, and as White gave his guests higher and higher swings in turn their legs touched the umbrella. It was an opulent decor with which White impressed his young guests and titillated his own senses.

White was much taken with the delightful Evelyn and sent her expensive and romantic presents, a feather boa and a red cape among them. He befriended her mother, and was always so much the gentleman that when Evelyn's mother went to Pittsburgh for a stay she had no qualms in accepting White's offer to take care of her daughter.

One night after appearing in *Floradora* Evelyn went by invitation to White's

Opposite
Evelyn Thaw, whose confession of a premarital affair prompted her husband's bloody vengeance.
Left
Stanford White, architect and murder victim.

apartment for a party but found him alone. There was champagne, there were back stairs to a bedroom with mirrors on walls and ceiling and, as Evelyn put it, she came to after the champagne to find White and herself naked together in bed.

The third actor in a triangle of jealousy which was to end, ironically, at the opening night of a musical was another man prominent in the public eye. He was Henry Kendall Thaw, a playboy and cocaine addict, whose father, William Thaw, had been an extremely rich railway magnate from Pittsburgh. The younger Thaw had left Harvard early to spend his time in club life and playing poker. Like White, he enjoyed parties, and was said to have spent $50,000 – then an enormous sum – on a party in Paris for his ne'er-do-well friends and the city's whores. Among his escapades was riding a horse into a club which had barred him. Because of his notorious activities, he was given only a small allowance from the $40 million estate on his father's death, but his mother continued to finance his wilful pursuits.

Thaw was quite handsome and, since very rich men generally get what they want (his whole fate was to be decided by his wealth), so Thaw got the delectable Evelyn Nesbit as a bride in 1905, when she was 20 and he was 33.

It was not a particularly happy relationship. They had lived together as man and wife before the wedding and had in fact made the headlines in New York when evicted from a hotel for cohabiting, she being a minor. During this time Evelyn had been badly treated by Thaw. He frequently beat her, and on one occasion in Europe, when she was still only 18, he had gone berserk, ripping her clothes from her and so belabouring her with a cowhide whip that it was three weeks before she could walk. She had sworn an affidavit about the incident to a New York lawyer, and thus was unable to conceal it when her husband's character was under attack at his trial.

Thaw had had all he wanted for over 30 years, but having gained possession of Evelyn Nesbit, he began to brood on her earlier seduction, when she was only 16, by White. It provoked him to murder.

There have been four Madison Square Gardens in the history of New York. Stanford White's was the second. Built on a block on the corner of Madison and Fourth Avenues and costing over $1\frac{1}{2}$ million in the 1890s, it was dominated by a 340-ft tower with a threatre roof garden where people sat at tables to enjoy the show and take refreshment. On 25 June 1906 New York's social set were watching a new musical, *Mamzelle Champagne*. They were not enjoying it, because it was rather bad. Indeed, one of the audience, Evelyn Nesbit, thought it so boring that she decided to leave, and made her way to the lobby with her husband and two of their guests. She did not notice at first that her husband had lagged behind.

Thaw had stopped at a table where Stanford White sat alone, having been promised by the stage manager that a particular chorus girl would be introduced to him after the show. Suddenly Thaw took

Top (inset)
Mrs Holman, Thaw's mother, who campaigned tirelessly on her son's behalf.

out a gun and, crying 'You have ruined my life', fired three shots at White, who slowly toppled to the floor, a bullet in his brain. The table and glasses fell with him and soon other tables went crashing as the New York socialites screamed and stampeded. The manager stood on one table to try to preserve order. Evelyn Nesbit rushed back saying, 'Good God, Harry, what have you done?', while Thaw, his gun held above his head, made his way to the exit. He was arrested and taken to a cell, where he was to have every comfort while awaiting trial.

The case became almost a contest between justice and money. Thaw's mother returned from England claiming she was ready to spend a million dollars to save her son. White's character was assassinated in a campaign led by a well-paid press agent. All sorts of stories were dug up about young girls seduced and ruined after a turn on the red velvet swing. There was even a play written giving a view of the 'murder', in which a Harold Daw shot a Stanford Black in a roof garden theatre and declared: 'No jury on earth will send me to

Left
Madison Square Park and Gardens early in the 20th century.
Below left (inset)
Henry (Harry) K. Thaw enjoying a prison meal in comfort after his arrest.

the chair ... for killing the man who defamed my wife'.

Thaw's trial lasted nearly three months, and the jury could not agree, seven opting for 'guilty' and five for 'not guilty on the grounds of insanity'. In 1908 a second trial found him insane, and he was committed to an asylum. Five years later he was 'rescued' and taken to Canada, but was subsequently brought back. Pressure from his family led to a third trial. On this occasion he was found not guilty and freed. Evelyn Nesbit immediately left him.

After only 18 months of freedom Thaw kidnapped and whipped a youth and was tried for this crime and found insane, but another court reversed this decision. Thaw's money had triumphed over justice, and he remained free and able to indulge his sadistic tastes until his death in 1947 at the age of 76.

THE DEVOTED MR ROBINSON AND HIS SON JOHN

The music hall friends of the doctor's wife were suspicious, and the ship's captain saw through his disguise.

The Daily Mirror

Page 3

THE MORNING JOURNAL WITH THE SECOND LARGEST NET SALE

No. 2,110. MONDAY, AUGUST 1, 1910 One Halfpenny.

END OF THE ATLANTIC CHASE: "DR." CRIPPEN, WHO WAS ARRESTED AT FATHER POINT, CANADA, YESTERDAY.

Above
A contemporary newspaper photograph of Crippen.

Anybody inventing a name for a murderer could do worse than choose 'Crippen'. It has a ring to it. Make it 'Dr Crippen' and it sounds like the title of the latest horror movie.

There was a Dr Hawley Harvey Crippen, of course, and circumstances have combined to make him one of the most famous murderers in history. The picture of him most frequently published shows a dapper man with staring eyes behind round, gold-rimmed spectacles – a man who looked as if he might have a sinister secret. Add the fact that he was the first murderer caught by a new invention, the wireless telegraph, to the accompaniment of great publicity, plus a victim from the music hall stage and a fleeing mistress dressed as a boy, and all the ingredients are there for a famous case. However, there are many who consider Dr Crippen was a wretched man deserving of sympathy rather than an evil one.

Crippen was born in Coldwater, Michigan, in 1862. He became a successful doctor, married, was widowed, and then fell in love with one of his patients, the vivacious 17-year-old Cora Turner. In her short life she had already lived with a man, been pregnant and miscarried, and the mild, short-statured Crippen no doubt found this outrageous behaviour, together with her gaiety and buxom charms, exciting. They married in 1893 and in 1900, when Crippen became manager of the English branch of a medicine company, they began living in London.

Cora had ambitions to be an operatic singer and Crippen had paid for her lessons. In London she switched her affection to the music hall, and took the stage name of Belle Elmore. Unfortunately, she was not very talented, but she found herself a role in working for the Music Hall Ladies Guild, where she could continue to act the part of the vaudeville star. She was highly popular, spent extravagantly on jewellery and, when her husband was away on a long trip, found herself a lover in a fellow-

American singer on the London stage, Bruce Miller. (Would Crippen have become as famous if he and the honest-sounding Bruce Miller had been born with each other's names?)

After five years in London, the Crippens moved into a desirable residence at 39 Hilldrop Crescent, on the woody northern fringes of the city. The rent was high, Cora began to take in 'guests' and Crippen, by now also a partner in a dental clinic, had more work to do in the evening, such as cleaning boots and humping coal. Cora had told him of the affair with Bruce Miller and now slept in a separate bedroom to her husband.

Crippen began to woo a quiet, gentle secretary at Munyons, the company whose office he managed, and eventually the two began a discreet affair. Ethel Le Neve, 24 years old and unmarried, was the opposite of Cora – demure, understanding and undemanding. She consoled Crippen in his unhappy marriage.

Cora learned of the affair and threatened to leave her husband. In November 1909 he lost his job as Munyon's manager, his arrangement with the company switching to a commission basis, and Cora decided to give the bank notice that she was withdrawing the £600 in her and Crippen's joint account.

In January 1910 Crippen bought five grains of a new drug called hyoscine. On the last day of the month the pair entertained to dinner and a game of whist Clara and Paul Martinetti, two retired music hall entertainers. They left at 1.30 am, whereupon, according to Crippen, his wife berated him for not devoting enough attention to the guests.

Hours afterwards Cora was dead from poisoning. Crippen was then able to remove her flesh from her bones, burn the bones and bury the flesh in the cellar, wrapped up in his pyjama jacket with quicklime. The day after dinner with the Martinettis, Crippen had already begun pawning Cora's jewellery. He sent Ethel Le Neve to the Music Hall Ladies Guild with a letter telling them that their treasurer had been called back urgently to the United States because of a relative's illness.

Left
Ethel Le Neve dressed as a boy.
Below left
Crippen's wife Cora, who took the stage name of Belle Elmore.

In answer to subsequent enquiries from Cora's friends, Crippen then invented an illness for his wife, and on 26 March 1910 they, and readers of *Era* magazine, were informed that Belle Elmore had died of pneumonia.

Crippen might well have got away with the crime, but the new happiness he and Ethel Le Neve enjoyed caused them to behave very recklessly. Ethel had moved into 39 Hilldrop Crescent, and she began

Above left (inset) **Captain Kendall, whose suspicions led to the arrest of Crippen.**
Above right (inset) **Detective Sergeant Mitchell and two wardresses at the start of their journey to Canada to bring back Crippen.**

appearing in public wearing Cora's jewellery. At the end of June music-hall friends of Cora's returned from California saying that no notice of Cora's death had appeared there. Scotland Yard was informed of the suspicious circumstances.

In July Chief Inspector Walter Dew called at Crippen's office, asking to see a death certificate. Crippen explained to him that his wife's death was an invention – she had, he said, returned to America to join a lover, probably Bruce Miller, and he had told the story to save her reputation and his embarrassment. He made a long statement, his house was searched and Inspector Dew was satisfied.

However, Crippen panicked. The next day, a Saturday, he and Ethel Le Neve fled to Europe. On Monday Chief Inspector Dew returned to the house with some

minor queries, found it empty and organized a more thorough search of the premises. Removal of a stone in the cellar floor revealed some rotting flesh, enough of which was left to show that it probably belonged to Cora and that it contained hyoscine. Warrants were issued for the arrest of Crippen and Le Neve, and descriptions were circulated.

The story now shifts to the ocean-going liner SS *Montrose*, which left Antwerp for Quebec on 20 July 1910. The commander, Captain Kendall, was keen on crime stories and knew the details of this latest gruesome murder, and also that the *Daily Mail* had offered £100 reward for news of the whereabouts of the runaways. Captain Kendall was soon keeping a watchful eye on two of his passengers, John Philo Robinson and his 16-year-old son, John. He thought the father was far too solicitous of his son's welfare, frequently even holding his hand. On the second day out he invited them to his table and his suspicions grew. The boy's trousers seemed too big and were oddly gathered by a safety pin. He radioed London that he believed Crippen and Le Neve were aboard.

Chief Inspector Dew set off for Quebec in a faster ship, while Captain Kendall watched the unsuspecting pair and radioed daily reports of their activities back to the eager *Daily Mail*, whose readers were highly diverted by this serial story of the impending capture of a murderer. On 31 July, less than a day out from Quebec, Dew boarded the *Montrose* at St Lawrence disguised as a ship's pilot. As Dew approached 'Robinson', one of the most famous meetings in the history of crime took place:

> *'Good morning, Dr Crippen. I am Chief Inspector Dew of Scotland Yard. I believe you know me'.*
> *'Good morning, Mr Dew'.*

Crippen was brought back to London for a trial in which he protested his innocence but was found guilty. He was hanged in Pentonville Prison on 23 November 1910, and was buried with Ethel Le Neve's letters and photograph. In a separate trial, she was found not guilty of being an accessory, the speech made by her counsel, F. E. Smith, being regarded as one of the classics of advocacy. She was freed and disappeared from the public view. Although people in general had shown the couple marked hostility, there were already a few discerning or romantic souls who felt sorry for the young 'John Robinson', and even for her over-attentive 'father'.

Left
Crippen and Le Neve in court. They were to be tried separately.

THE MAN WHO STOLE THE MONA LISA

For two years the world's most famous painting was missing, while an Italian patriot wore its enigmatic smile.

A police photograph of Vincenzo Perruggia.

There can be little doubt about which is the most famous painting in the world: the one known either as the 'Mona Lisa' or 'La Gioconda', and painted by Leonardo da Vinci in Florence around 1503–06. Should it come on the market today, it is impossible to guess what price it might fetch, but, of course, the sale of the greatest art treasure of the Louvre in Paris is unthinkable.

Imagine the horror and disbelief in the Louvre on 22 August 1911 when it dawned on the authorities that the famous painting was missing. The blank space on the wall had been first noticed about 8.35 am on 21 August, a day on which the gallery was closed to the public, but nobody took any action. The assumption was that it was being photographed somewhere in the building – a not uncommon occurrence. However, the following morning, when visitors began to ask where it was, the gallery staff became increasingly interested in its whereabouts until, halfway through the day, the absence of the Mona Lisa was brought to the attention of the director and then of the police. The whole gallery was searched by an army of policemen. The frame was found on a staircase, but of the painting itself there was no sign.

The French were scandalized. Rumours sped through Paris. The head curator of the Louvre was sacked and the government minister responsible forced to resign. Police activity was frenetic, and for a while it was unsafe to appear in a Paris street with a parcel – a gendarme would be sure to pounce. Even Pablo Picasso was arrested on suspicion.

None of this activity, however, produced any results. For the next two years nothing was heard of the Mona Lisa and the world began to think that Leonardo's masterpiece might never be seen again.

During this time the only man who knew where the Mona Lisa was to be found was an Italian carpenter, Vincenzo Perruggia. Perruggia had been one of the four men employed by the Louvre in 1910 to reframe the painting and put it under glass. Consequently he knew exactly how it was hung. He continued visiting the gallery after his employment was terminated, and one day he attended wearing the white blouse of the gallery's workmen, some of whom he knew. He found he could come in and out without arousing attention. One morning he entered the room containing the picture when it was empty. Quickly taking it from the wall, he carried it to a staircase, where he just as quickly removed the frame and, with the painting under his blouse, strolled out of the gallery. He took the painting to his lodgings, where he kept it under the bed.

The empty space left after the theft of the Mona Lisa.

The Paris police might well have been incompetent, but they were sensible enough to interview the hundreds who had worked at the Louvre during the previous few years. They spoke to Perruggia in his room, perhaps even sat on the bed below which the painting was concealed. However, they did not take his fingerprints. If they had done so they might have discovered that his left thumb print tallied with that found on the glass of the missing painting. Actually, they had his thumb print on file, because he had been in trouble in 1909, but only the thumb print of the right hand was recorded, so there was no point in checking that.

In November 1913 an art dealer in Florence received a letter from Paris in which the writer offered to send him the greatest painting in the world, which he (the writer) had stolen. The painting had been stolen so that it could be returned to Florence, its rightful home. The art dealer showed the letter to the director of the Uffizi Gallery, and the two men invited the writer, 'Leonard', who was really Perruggia, to Florence. He arrived at the art dealer's office without the painting but,

Top
The Mona Lisa under guard at the Uffizi Gallery in Florence after its recovery.
Right
The painting is returned to the French ambassador in Rome.

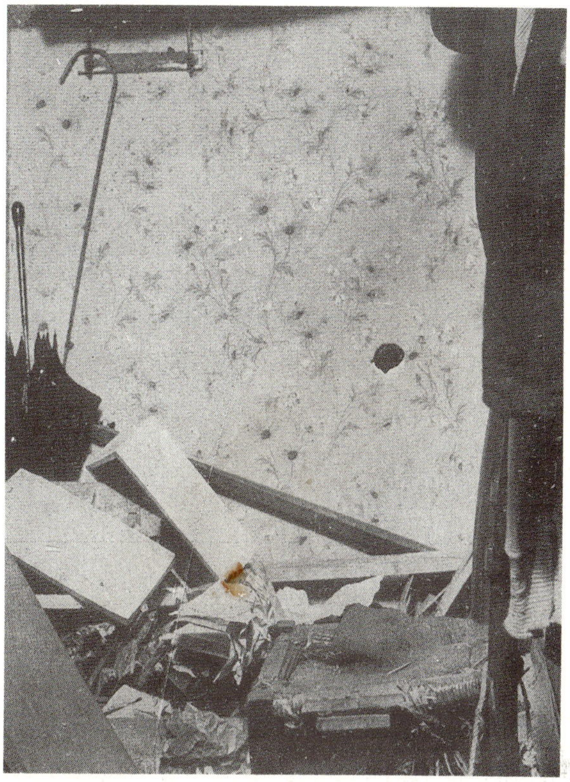

Perruggia's lodgings in Paris where the stolen masterpiece remained hidden for two years.

after the sum of 500,000 lire had been mentioned, he agreed to return.

Next day, the two men were invited to Perruggia's cheap hotel, the Tripoli-Italia. From a trunk full of everyday objects under the bed, Perruggia produced the Mona Lisa, wrapped in red silk.

The whole affair was too big to remain a secret, of course. Perruggia was arrested and the Mona Lisa, after incredulous officials in Paris had been persuaded to believe the story, was returned to the Louvre, surrounded by armed guards. But before this thousands of emotional Italians saw it in the Uffizi Gallery, and it was also shown in Rome and Milan.

Perruggia, the man who brought the Mona Lisa back to Italy, was a hero to his countrymen. His trial centred on the question of whether he had stolen the painting for patriotic reasons or for financial gain. There was much discussion about who had raised the subject of money in his first talk with the art dealer and gallery director in Florence. Unfortunately, there had also been a trip to London and a talk to a dealer who had, allegedly, not taken seriously Perruggia's attempts to sell the painting.

There was stony silence when the prosecutor asked for three years' imprisonment, but the courtroom applause for the defending counsel's speech was more in keeping with La Scala, and when it was taken up by crowds outside the courtroom, Perruggia burst into tears.

Nevertheless, Perruggia was found guilty of theft and sentenced to a year and 15 days in prison. However, this was reduced to seven months on appeal and, since he had been held for seven months already, he was released. He returned to the Tripoli-Italia hotel to find it was now called La Gioconda and sported a reproduction of the famous painting in the foyer. Unfortunately, Perruggia could still afford only the cheapest room, although, of course, he was received like a hero.

NEARER, MY GOD, TO THEE

The saucy bigamist nipped out for the supper while his wife took her bath, but he did it once too often.

Fiction writers are often accused of excessive use of coincidence in developing their plots, especially when everything depends on two characters meeting in an unlikely place. Yet the career of one of the most famous of all murderers was launched on just such a coincidence.

When Henry Williams wooed and won a well-off young woman in Weymouth, a seaside town in Dorset, in August 1910, and then disappeared a few weeks later, taking with him all the money he could get his hands on from her trust fund, she hardly expected to see him again. He wrote to her saying he had contracted a terrible disease from her, and that a long cure was necessary before he could return. Mrs Williams joined a friend in lodgings in Weston-super-Mare, over 50 miles from Weymouth and, in those days, almost a different part of the country. How surprised she must have been one day 18 months or so later when, walking along the sea front, she bumped into her husband.

She accosted him, but instead of recriminations there was a joyful reconciliation and she immediately moved into his lodgings. Soon the couple went off to begin life together anew in Herne Bay.

This proved to be a terrible mistake on the part of the gullible Mrs Williams, who could see no connection between three events which took place in one week in July 1912, soon after they arrived in Herne Bay: Mr Williams bought and installed in the house a second-hand bath; he and his wife made wills in each other's favour; and he took her to a Dr French to seek advice about her 'fits' – although these were a surprise to her, as she felt quite well.

Alas, the fourth event of the week was her death. Dr French was summoned by a note to the lodgings to find her in the bath, her head under the water, drowned. She was still holding a bar of soap in her hand. Mr Williams, it appeared, had been out buying fish when she died. There was an inquest, at which Williams wept continuously. Dr French gave his opinion that Mrs Williams had had an epileptic seizure in the bath, causing her to fall back and drown. Mr Williams came into a legacy of £2,571, which he invested in houses and a shop in Bristol, and in buying himself an annuity.

Now it might not be unusual for a woman to die in her bath, but it would if the tragedy occurred the day after her wedding day and this unfortunate fate befell a clergyman's daughter, Margaret Lofty, from Bath, who married a John Lloyd on 17 December 1914. They arrived that same day in their new lodgings in Highgate, London, and in the evening Mr Lloyd took his wife to see a local doctor about her 'fits'. Mrs Lloyd had already insured her life (Mr Lloyd paid the first premium) and next morning put her financial affairs in order by accompanying her husband of one day to a solicitor's office where she made a will in his favour.

That night she was having a bath – the landlady heard splashing sounds. A few minutes later she also heard Mr Lloyd in the front room playing on the harmonium the hymn 'Nearer, My God, to Thee'. Ten minutes later Mr Lloyd was ringing the front doorbell, telling the landlady that he had slipped out to buy some tomatoes for his wife's supper and had forgotten his keys. Alas, on going upstairs he found that Mrs Lloyd was dead, having drowned in her bath.

There was an inquest on 1 January 1915, over a week after the funeral, and the coroner came to the routine conclusion that Mrs Lloyd had drowned after having fainted. This was just the sort of story that *News of the World* readers liked on a Sunday morning, and the editor thought that 'Bride's Tragic Fate on Day after Wedding' was good enough for the front page.

Two readers, one in Buckinghamshire and the other in Blackpool, read this story and contacted the police.

One was the father of Alice Burnham, a buxom 25-year-old private nurse, who had married a George Smith at Portsmouth in November 1913, a year before Mrs Lloyd's sad death. The day before the wedding Mr Smith had taken out a £500 insurance policy on his future wife's life, and immediately afterwards he had written to Mr Burnham asking for £104 which Mr Burnham was looking after on behalf of his daughter. Having obtained possession of it, through a solicitor, he took his wife to Blackpool where, in the lodgings of a Mrs Crossley, she too had drowned in her bath. The verdict at the inquest was that she had fainted. Mr Burnham thought that the similarity between the two cases was sufficient to warrant police enquiries.

The other person to contact the police was the Blackpool landlady herself, Mrs Crossley. She told them of running a bath for Mrs Smith while the couple took a walk. Mrs Crossley was having a meal when she and her husband found water coming through the ceiling from above. At that moment Smith knocked at the front door with some eggs he had 'just popped out to buy for breakfast', and Mrs Crossley, indicating the water, told him to hurry upstairs. What he found we know. At the inquest a tearful Smith was not pressed too hard on why he had not attempted to lift his wife out of the bath or remove the plug.

Mrs Crossley was so incensed at Smith's

callousness in allowing only the cheapest of funerals and in playing the piano while awaiting the inquest – the tunes are not recorded – that when he left she called him 'Crippen' and wrote on his card: 'We shall see him again'.

The police investigated 'Mr Smith' and 'Mr Lloyd', and discovered 'Mr Williams' and a host of other aliases, together with

Far left
George Joseph Smith, whose eyes exercised a hypnotic charm over some women.
Below left
Edith Pegler, one of the women whom Smith bigamously married. He was apparently quite fond of her and she survived.

disappointed brides and fiancées, all belonging to the same man.

George Joseph Smith, for that was his real name, was born in Bethnal Green, London, in 1872. At nine he was sent to a reformatory and, apart from a short career in the army, he alternated spells in prison with life as a thief. His hypnotic eyes made women easy prey for him, and in 1898, as 'George Love', he married the 18-year-old Caroline Thornhill. She took work as a servant in wealthy houses, but in 1899 was convicted and imprisoned for theft. Smith disappeared, but on her release she met him (by coincidence again) in London and had him imprisoned for receiving.

Before Smith met Beatrice Mundy, the first 'bride in the bath', whom he married as Henry Williams, he had already contracted at least three other bigamous marriages, abandoning all his wives except one once he had got his hands on their possessions. The one he 'kept' was Edith Pegler, whom he married in 1908 and to whom he returned in Bristol in the intervals between his other adventures. So far as she was concerned, his absences were prompted by a search for antiques.

Three months before the death which inspired the investigations, Smith had married another girl and relieved her of her savings. Those brides who did not die in baths he left in public places, such as the National Gallery, asking them to wait

Alice Burnham. Her father's suspicions about her untimely end led to police investigations.

while he went to the lavatory, never to reappear.

Although charged with three murders, Smith could, by law, be tried for only one, and the crux of the trial was whether or not the judge would permit reference to be made to the other two in order to establish that Smith operated a system. The judge did permit it, and Smith was doomed. It was suggested by the pathologist that his method of killing his brides was simple – he merely lifted their legs with one arm while pushing their heads under with the other. A nurse who submitted to a police 're-construction' was nearly overcome herself, and required energetic reviving.

The jury took 22 minutes to find Smith guilty and he was hanged at Maidstone Prison on 13 August 1915. His only legal wife, Caroline Thornhill, remarried the following day.

Although an evil man, Smith had a certain intelligence and wit. The solemn playing of 'Nearer My God to Thee' while his 'wife' drowned suggests a feeling for style, especially as only he could appreciate the joke. And when the father of his second 'bride' wanted to know about his parentage before parting with the £104 mentioned earlier, Smith replied:

> *Sir, In answer to your application regarding my parentage, my mother was a bus-horse, my father a cab-driver, my sister a rough rider over Arctic regions. My brothers were all gallant sailors on a steam-roller. This is the only information I can give to those who are not entitled to ask such questions contained in the letter I received on the 24th inst. Your despised son-in-law, G. Smith.*

Most of all perhaps, his remark to his 'regular wife', Edith, on his return from one of the inquests, shows his self-sufficient wit. 'Don't buy a bath,' he said, 'as it is well-known that women often lose their lives through weak hearts and fainting in a bath'. When she related this at his trial he was visibly upset.

Above left
Margaret Lofty. As 'Mrs Lloyd' she had the extreme misfortune to be drowned in her bath the day after her wedding.
Above right
Beatrice Mundy, Smith's first victim, had a substantial private income.

The 1920s

Bluebeard,
a lethal seduction,
a minister and a mistress,
adulterous couples and
a motiveless murder.

Albert Snyder's body being carried from his Long Island home.

BLUEBEARD'S LAST VICTIM

He had a way with women, as his little black book proved, but unfortunately many of them could not be found.

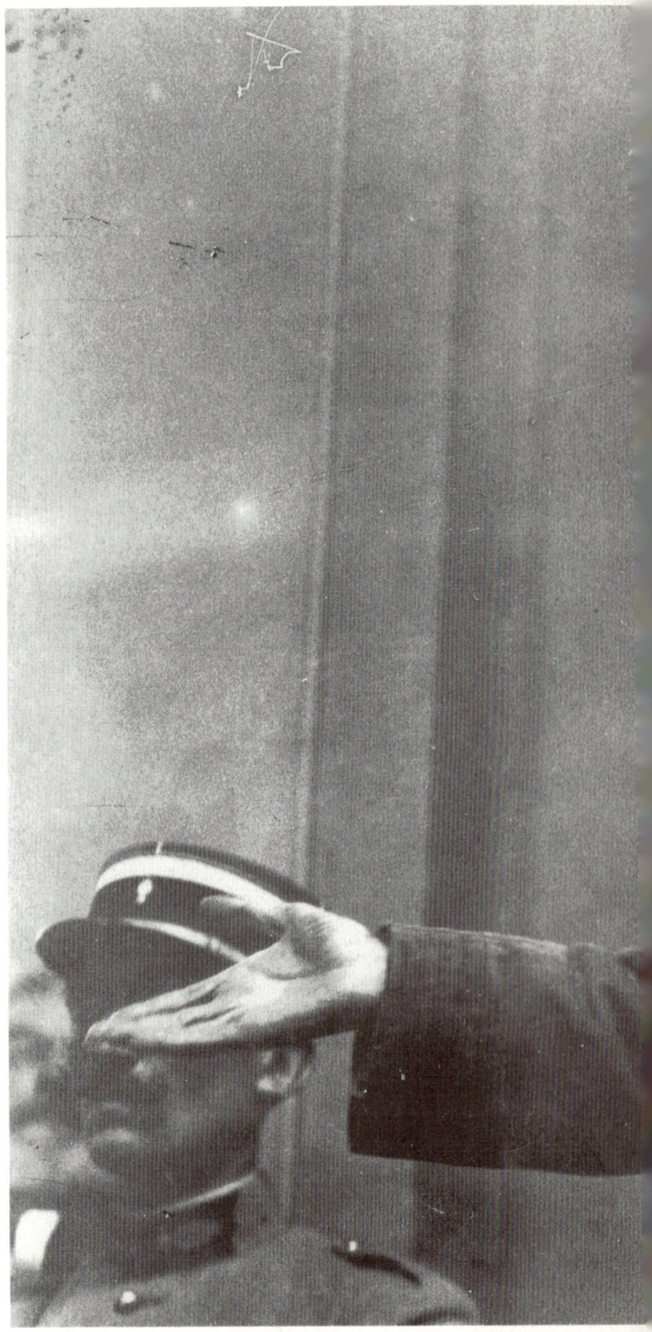

On 11 April 1919 an attractive, 29-year-old woman was shopping in the rue de Rivoli, in Paris, with her fiancé, a well-to-do engineer called Lucien Guillet. At least that was the name by which she knew him. A Mademoiselle Lacoste, who saw them together, knew him as Monsieur Dupont, and was aware that a warrant for his arrest had been issued the day before. She went to the police, an action which not only possibly saved the life of the young woman, Fernande Segret, but 50 years later won her 10,000 francs in libel damages.

The police discovered that Guillet had ordered a white china dinner service to be delivered to his apartment at 76, rue de Rochefouart. They went there and arrested him on a charge of murder, for Guillet was really Henri Désiré Landru. Among all his names the one by which he became world famous was a nickname: Bluebeard. This had originally been applied to a 16th-century child killer – Landru's beard was actually red.

Landru was born in Paris on 12 April 1869 of a good family. Clever at school, he became for a while a sub-deacon, but strayed from the straight and narrow path when seducing the daughter of his cousin. Two years after the birth of his own daughter he married the mother and had three other children. He worked as a clerk, an agent, a salesman and at various other occupations before he began adding to his income by sexual conquests.

His method was simple. He placed advertisements in Paris newspapers claiming to be a well-off, affectionate widower in his forties, with two children, seeking a widow with a view to matrimony.

One woman who replied was a Madame Celestine Buisson, who later visited the advertiser, a Monsieur Dupont, in his house, the Villa Ermitage, at Gambais, near Paris. Madame Buisson disappeared, and her worried sister, Mademoiselle Lacoste (who later saw 'Dupont' shopping) wrote to the mayor at Gambais asking for help in tracing her.

Just before this letter arrived, the mayor had received another from a Madame Pelat. This lady also had a sister, a 44-year-old widow, Madame Collomb, and she, too, had answered an advertisement and had disappeared. This advertisement was

Left
Landru in court. He maintained a remarkable composure until the very end.
Below left
Landru in a wedding group with Fernande Segret.

placed by a Monsieur Cuchet. Madame Collomb went to live with Cuchet in his flat in the rue Chateaudun. He took her to visit his house at Gambais, where she discovered he was known as Monsieur Fremyet. On Christmas Eve 1916 the couple took Madame Pelat to see the Gambais villa.

When the mayor received his two letters, he put Mademoiselle Lacoste and Madame Pelat in touch with each other and the two women, who had each lost a sister, decided that Cuchet-Fremyet and Dupont were the same man. It now transpired that Cuchet was the name of a woman who had disappeared with her son

Right
A witness giving evidence during Landru's trial, which lasted three weeks.
Below
Landru, with photographs of some of his victims. The true total can only be guessed at.

after going to live with a Monsieur Diard at Vernouillet, near Paris.

Convinced that the names Cuchet, Fremyet, Dupont and Diard belonged to one man, the police issued a warrant for his arrest. The next day he was seen shopping by Mademoiselle Lacoste and, as related, apprehended.

When arrested, Landru, the owner of all the names, threw a black notebook through his window. It was recovered and found to contain lists of matrimonial advertisements he had placed and replies to them, together with notes of those responses worth following up in respect of possible fortunes. There was also a careful account of his day-to-day spending, with significant details (so far as Celestine Buisson and Anna Collomb were concerned) such as the purchase of one return ticket and one single ticket on their last trips to Gambais.

Landru was discovered to have two flats in Paris and houses at Gambais and Vernouillet, as well as a garage at Clichy, where his wife and four children lived.

As police investigated the activities of Landru, they found stoves at Gambais and Vernouillet, and neighbours to testify that black, evil-smelling smoke had frequently been emitted from them – the local police at Gambais had indeed spoken to him after complaints about it. Articles of women's clothing and jewellery were found there, and more were discovered at his Paris flats. Of the actual victims there was no trace. Police pieced together the gruesome theory that Landru killed them, cut them up and burned them.

Landru's notebook helped police to identify 283 women with whom he had had 'dealings', and the names of ten whom he was alleged to have disposed of were read out in court. Madame Cuchet's son was an 11th victim. Most were widowed or divor-

Left
Closely guarded in his cell, Landru awaits the jury's verdict.

ced women whose possessions Landru had appropriated, as his notebook showed.

Landru's trial was something of a knockabout affair, with wolf whistles and catcalls from the public. Landru himself maintained an impressive dignity, and asserted to the end that, while he had cheated these women, he had killed none. With the evidence almost wholly circumstantial, many believed him.

A star witness was Fernande Segret, with whom he had ordered the dinner service he was never to use. She testified that sexual relations with him were quite normal, and the medical evidence was that he was sane. The jury took $1\frac{1}{2}$ hours to find him guilty of the murders, and he was executed on the guillotine, watched by a crowd of curious spectators. Strangely, the prosecutor was absent. Landru had written to him accusing him of judicial murder, which apparently considerably disturbed him.

And Mademoiselle Segret's 10,000 francs? When a film of Landru's life was released in the 1960s she reappeared and sued for damages. Everybody had assumed she was dead. However the 10,000-franc award did her no good, for she found herself again a centre of attention in relation to Landru, could not face it and drowned herself. It might be said that Bluebeard had claimed his last victim from beyond the grave.

'LET ME CALL YOU SWEETHEART'

Everybody laughed at the fat man, but his private life did not match his slapstick movie image.

Roscoe Arbuckle with Buster Keaton, who proved a loyal friend.

Roscoe 'Fatty' Arbuckle was born (weighing 16½ lb) in 1887 in South Center, Kansas, and after appearing in vaudeville made some one- and two-reeler films. In 1913 Mack Sennett engaged him at $3 a day to become one of the famous Keystone Cops of silent comedy. His career took off and he appeared in many films with the up-and-coming Charlie Chaplin. When Chaplin left the Sennett studio, 'Fatty' Arbuckle was promoted to star in many films with Mabel Normand, films with titles like *Mabel and Fatty's Married Life*. In 1917 Arbuckle was able to join the famous Players–Lasky studio at $7,000 a week and by 1921 was making his own films, becoming second in popularity only to Chaplin.

Virginia Rappe. Her rejection of Arbuckle's advances ended in tragedy.

In September 1921 Arbuckle threw a party in the St Francis Hotel, San Francisco. It was a boisterous affair, with a plentiful supply of girls, for Arbuckle, separated from his wife, was known to have a sexual appetite on the same scale as his 250-lb frame. He claimed he lived only for women. In fact he was also known to be violent, and complaints had been lodged against him by girls on whom he had tried to force his favours.

Arbuckle, no doubt because of his appearance, often found the women he fancied hard to get, and was known to obtain particular pleasure from the sexual conquest of a girl who had at first shown herself indifferent to, or even repelled by, him. One such was the 25-year-old Virginia Rappe, a bit-player and 'girl-around-Hollywood'. She had resisted Arbuckle for some five years. On the day of the party she was staying in the nearby Palace Hotel, with her agent and a friend, and as Arbuckle's party went on from morning to evening, and the champagne and music began to go flat, Arbuckle rang her and invited her round. Virginia came because she wanted to star in one of his pictures, and she brought her agent with her.

Virginia Rappe was a beautiful girl, whose face appeared on the sheet music of the popular song 'Let Me Call You Sweetheart'. Whether or not she was prepared to pay the traditional 'I can make you a star' price that night, she soon found herself in his bedroom. Witnesses said she was hustled in by the gloating Arbuckle who boasted that now he had what he had waited five years for.

However, screams were soon heard from behind the locked door, screams so frightening that the hotel manager was sent for. As he arrived Arbuckle emerged from the bedroom wearing Virginia's hat

Above
A sombre-faced Arbuckle in court. The jury failed to agree in the first two trials.
Below
Arbuckle with relatives and members of the jury after his acquittal.

and dancing in glee. Behind him, among her ripped clothes, Virginia lay on the floor moaning. 'Roscoe hurt me', she said, 'I'm dying'. Arbuckle showed no remorse for whatever it was he had done, calling her a lousy actress and threatening to throw her out of the window.

The hotel doctor arrived, and had Virginia taken to another room. Then, four days later, he transferred her to a private clinic where she died soon after being admitted. The deputy coroner of San Francisco found a ruptured bladder and called the police. An inquest recorded that

A still from the film *Close Relations*. Despite his acquittal Arbuckle's career was virtually over.

Arbuckle was criminally responsible for the death and he was charged with murder.

At the preliminary hearing the allegations concerning Virginia's death were written down as they were considered too terrible to be read out, but Arbuckle's friends were questioned privately and rumours circulated that he had used an ice-pick on her or perhaps, enraged at her coolness, had rammed ice into her genitals.

Arbuckle's story at the trial proper was that he had accidentally crushed her by his weight during intercourse. So far as the ice was concerned, he claimed he had merely placed ice on her thigh after she had complained of feeling sick.

The jury were divided at his first trial and again at the second. At the third he was acquitted. There are suspicions that the Hollywood film interests had bribed some of the jury, who declared: 'Acquittal is not enough for Roscoe Arbuckle. We feel a great injustice has been done to him. . . .'

If what the jury said was true, it certainly was a great injustice, for Arbuckle's career was as good as over. A funny fat man is not funny any more if his audience believe he is a monster, and he was called the 'fat killer'. The public boycotted his films, and exhibitors gave up showing them, writing off $500,000 for the studio in unshown stock. Arbuckle tried to return to the stage but was booed wherever he went, including places as far away as Paris. Some stood by him, notably Buster Keaton, and he remarried. He directed films under a pseudonym – William B. Goodrich – and in 1932 Warner Brothers engaged him to make twelve comedies. But the first ones were bad and were, anyway, banned in Britain. Arbuckle died in 1933 before completing them.

Hollywood is a place where sex scandals have become common. But Arbuckle's was the first, and occurred in comparatively innocent times. Nevertheless, there is probably some truth in his remark that, had he been tall, dark and handsome, rather than fat, foolish and moon-faced, he would have got away with it.

THE MINISTER AND THE SEXTON'S WIFE

The smart prosecutor could not break Crazy Willie, and the defendants in the sensational murder trial were acquitted.

On 16 September 1922, under a crab-apple tree in a lovers' lane near the River Raritan on the outskirts of New Brunswick, New Jersey, a courting couple were presented with a horrific tableau. The bodies of a man and woman were lying side by side, her head on his arm and her hand on his knee. The bodies had been deliberately arranged and, as if it were a label in a museum, the man's calling card was propped up against his shoe, revealing him as the Rev. Edward W. Hall, rector of the Protestant Episcopal Church of St John the Evangelist in New Brunswick. After the alarm had been raised and the bodies examined, it was discovered that both victims had been shot in the head. Moreover, the woman's throat had been slashed from ear to ear and her tongue and vocal chords cut out. When the scarf hiding the wound was removed, a seething mass of maggots was seen. The bodies had been there for about 36 hours and, on the ground around them, were two cartridge cases and several passionate love-letters addressed to the minister by Mrs Eleanor Mills, a choir singer at the church and the wife of his sexton. Mrs Mills was the female victim.

It was well known locally that the 41-year-old minister, several years younger than his wife, and Mrs Mills who, in her early thirties was also much younger than her husband, were having an affair, and the police closely questioned the minister's wife, Mrs Frances Hall, and her two brothers, Willie and Henry Stevens. But the only convincing evidence against them was that of Jane Gibson, a woman who kept pigs and who was, unfortunately, to become famous as the 'Pig Woman'. She lived near by and explained that, since she was on the lookout for thieves who were taking her Indian corn, on the night of the murder, when her dog barked, she went to investigate. Her story was that two women and two men were arguing by the crab-apple tree. A white-haired woman was demanding an explanation of some letters. She saw something gleam in the hand of one man and heard four shots. A woman screamed, and another said 'Oh, Henry!' – and then she (Jane Gibson) fled on her mule. But, like Cinderella, she had dropped her moccasin, and three hours later returned for it. There were no bodies, but she did see the white-haired woman kneeling in the lane weeping. From photographs she recognized her as Mrs Hall and

Above right
Mrs Frances Hall, the murdered minister's wife, was charged with the crime, together with her brothers.

Left
Spectators leaving Somerville county courthouse where the murder trial was being held.
Below left
Willie Stevens being led to jail under guard.

her bushy-haired brother Willie as one of the men present on the first occasion.

At a preliminary hearing which investigated the evidence a grand jury decided that there was insufficient evidence to indict Mrs Hall and her brothers. There the matter rested for four years, although the press tried to keep the case alive.

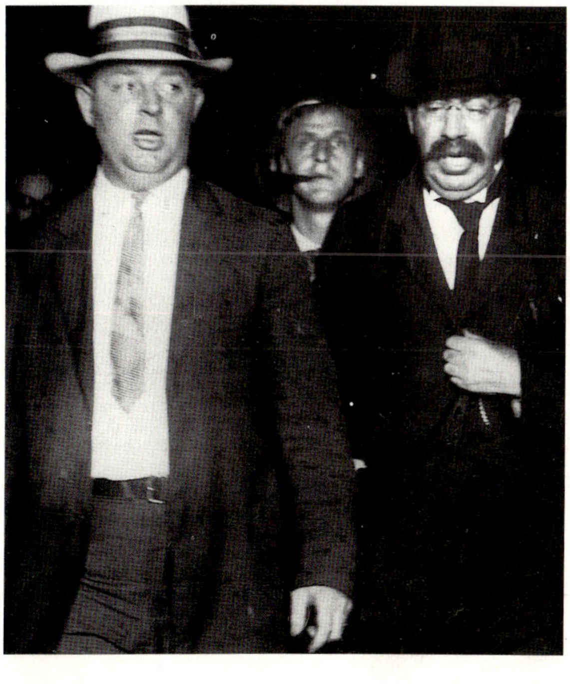

The whole matter erupted again when one Arthur Riehl was seeking an annulment of his marriage to the former Miss Louise Geist. Miss Geist had been a parlourmaid of the Halls at the time of the murders, and Riehl testified that his wife had claimed that 'she knew all about the case but had been given $5,000 to hold her tongue'. Mrs Hall and her family were extremely wealthy. The story was seized upon by the New York *Daily Mirror*, which provoked the authorities into reopening the case.

Mrs Hall and her brothers, Willie and Henry, were charged with the crime. Their cousin, Henry de la Bruyere Carpender, who had arranged the minister's funeral and had been reported hanging about the scene of the murder a year later, was charged with complicity.

The trial opened on 3 November 1926, the public once more showing a tremendous interest in these larger-than-life characters and the strange and terrible crime which had brought them into prominence.

The exhumation of the body of Mrs Eleanor Mills just before the beginning of the trial.

The case was predicted to rest upon an expected duel between Willie Stevens, an ungainly, shambling, eccentric man with prominent, blinking eyes behind thick spectacles, who was popularly regarded as something of an oddity – he was even called in the press 'Crazy Willie' – and the smart, forceful prosecutor, Senator Alexander Simpson. The latter, not known for handling witnesses gently, let it be known that he intended to 'tie Willie Stevens into knots', and settle the question once and for all.

However, before these two came face to face, the prosecution's case had not gone well. The parlourmaid whose supposed knowledge had set the trial in motion declared her husband's allegations were nonsense. On the contrary, she said, he had married her principally to find out the secret of the murders and, on discovering that she knew nothing, had made his assertions out of spite.

After this it was announced that the Pig Woman was in hospital with a serious kidney illness and would not be able to attend court. However, she was brought in on a stretcher and gave evidence in a weak voice. She retold her story, but the defence had located her mother, and found her a

prominent seat in court. The Pig Woman's quiet account no doubt lost some of its value as her mother loudly repeated: 'She's a liar. She always has been.'

The dignified Mrs Hall gave evidence that she did not even know of the affair between her husband and the choir singer (for whom she was paying a medical bill for an operation), and that on the fatal night she had searched for her husband with her brother Willie before alerting her lawyer to his disappearance.

Before Willie was called to the box, a doctor gave evidence that, although he was not absolutely normal mentally, he was in

Left
Charlotte Mills, daughter of Eleanor Mills, on the witness stand.

It has been suggested that the Ku Klux Klan may have had a hand in the killings.

fact of above average intelligence and read advanced books on subjects which interested him, such as metallurgy. Willie did not work for a living, having an allowance from a trust fund set up by his parents. He was known to have a great interest in the local fire brigade, frequently visiting the firehouse, sometimes taking a chicken or steak and treating the whole brigade to dinner. He had bought an expensive banner for the firemen's parades, which he himself joined as a kind of honorary member.

Willie Stevens got his age wrong in an early question, saying he was 44 instead of 54, but in the cross-examination he delighted those present in the courthouse with his replies, often correcting the prosecutor on his pronunciation or details of fact, for example pointing out that the deceased was not Doctor Hall but the Rev. Mr Hall. Far from destroying the credibility of the witness, the prosecutor found the case against Willie Stevens and, by implication, the others dissolving in the laughter of the spectators at his own discomfiture. Convinced that Willie had learned his account of the crucial evening by rote, Simpson had him repeat it and then, amidst vehement objections by the defence, overruled by the judge, asked him to go through it a third time. However, he abandoned this as soon as it became clear that Stevens could retell the story in different words and would not be shaken from it and, moreover, he let the prosecutor know that he, Willie, was well aware of what he was trying to do. After five hours' deliberation, the jury returned a verdict of 'not guilty' and all the prisoners were released.

The trial revealed bungling throughout by almost all the authorities connected with the case, beginning with the first investigators on the scene, men from Middlesex County. Realizing the site was, in fact, just over the border in Somerset County, they had retired and, by the time the scene of the crime was properly examined, the public and press had trampled it. Even the famous crab-apple tree had disappeared, removed bit by bit by souvenir hunters. Most of the officials concerned found their careers at a standstill. The New York *Daily Mirror* settled a $2 million libel claim by the defendants out of court for $50,000, and Philip Payne, the paper's managing editor, set off on a transatlantic flight to Rome as a stunt to retrieve his and the paper's reputation. He and the plane disappeared.

The murderers were never found. In the closing speech for the defence at the trial the Pig Woman was accused. The husband of Mrs Mills, James Mills the sexton, who had been a suspect himself, voiced a view shared by some others when he said that money could buy anything – Mrs Hall was the richest woman in New Brunswick and the implication was clear. A more recent theory, put forward by a lawyer, William Kunstler, is that the Ku Klux Klan killed the couple in retaliation for their blatant violation of the Klan's rules concerning sexual morality, the brutal removal of the singer's vocal chords being typical of their methods.

The Pig Woman died of her illness, and Mrs Hall went to her grave soon afterwards. Willie lived on to 1942.

CONVICTED BY CORRESPONDENCE

Some said she died for love. It could be said she died by her own hand – the hand that held her pen.

Far left
Frederick Bywaters, a photograph taken only a few days before the murder.
Left
Percy Thompson, the murder victim, in wartime uniform.

Lovers who are separated often convey their feelings for each other in letters. Sometimes these letters become passionate and full of nonsenses. Those of Edith Thompson were subject to the scrutiny of lawyers, judge and jury, and their impropriety put her on trial for her life.

Edith, a bookkeeper at a wholesale millinery company in the City of London, married Percy Thompson, a shipping clerk at the same firm, in 1915. Their married life seemed contented enough until 1921, when they went on an August bank holiday trip to the Isle of Wight in a party which included Frederick Bywaters. He was a handsome, husky and opinionated 19-year-old steward on an ocean liner, the SS *Morea*. He was eight years younger than Edith and 12 years younger than Percy. He and Edith took a liking to each other and, after the holiday, he came to live as a lodger in the Thompson home in Ilford. However, Percy became suspicious of his intentions and after a row Bywaters left.

Soon Bywaters asked Thompson to give his wife grounds to get a divorce, but Thompson refused; so Bywaters and Edith began a secret affair. In September, after much hand-holding at tea-dances and snatched kisses, they finally became lovers.

A year later, on 3 October 1922, during one of Bywaters' periods ashore, the couple met for afternoon tea in a shop in London. Edith then had to leave because her husband was taking her to the theatre. After the theatre, the Thompsons were

Below left
Edith Thompson seated between her lover (left) and her husband.

Right
Bywaters at Ilford Station after his arrest on a charge of murdering Percy Thompson.

walking home from the station along Belgrave Road, Ilford, when Bywaters appeared and began quarrelling with Thompson. Suddenly he took a knife from his pocket (sailors in those days frequently carried knives) and stabbed Thompson several times in the neck, chest and shoulders.

Edith cried: 'Oh don't! Oh don't!' but Thompson sank dying to the gutter, while a hysterical Edith screamed for help. A doctor and the police arrived, but too late to save her husband. Edith said he had been attacked by a strange man, who had fled.

It was a neighbour, who lived in the same house as the Thompsons, who told the police of Bywaters and his row with Percy. Police went to Bywaters' ship and found some of Edith's letters. Others were discovered at his mother's house. Eventually they found Bywaters himself, at the house of Edith Thompson's parents. After questioning he was charged with murder and, later, Edith, too, was charged. On catching sight of Bywaters at the police station, she cried: 'Oh God, why did he do it? I didn't want him to do it.'

Bywaters' defence at their trial was that Thompson had attacked him first after he had stopped him to press once again for a divorce, and that he thought Thompson, who threatened to shoot him, had a gun. Nothing could budge him from this version. He denied that at tea that afternoon he and Edith had planned the attack and he insisted that Edith had not known that he intended to waylay her husband.

Edith Thompson's counsel, Sir Henry Curtis-Bennett, tried to persuade the judge, in the absence of the jury, that Edith's letters should not be admitted in evidence unless the prosecution could show that she took part in the 'murder', but he was overruled. Edith was charged with being a principal in the second degree, the prosecution's case against her being that she conceived the crime and incited Bywaters to execute it.

No fewer than 62 of Edith's letters were placed in evidence by the prosecution, showing what a prolific writer she had been in little more than a year. She bravely (her counsel later said, foolishly) elected to go into the witness box to answer the prosecutor about several damning passages that were read out to her.

She addressed Bywaters in the letters as 'darlint' (representing 'darlingest') and several times seemed to describe how she was trying to kill her husband with poison and powdered glass. She talked of using an electric light globe and of the glass being

Left
Sir Henry Curtis-Bennett, who defended Edith Thompson at her trial.

not too powdered – in fact on one occasion she wrote about Thompson's finding a piece. She also sent Bywaters lots of suggestive newspaper cuttings about poisoners. She insisted that Bywaters feel jealousy: 'He has the right by law to all that you have the right by nature and love'. She also urged Bywaters to 'send (her) something', as she explained in court 'to make her husband ill'.

It all pointed in a terrible direction, but her counsel claimed that she was an extraordinary woman who lived in a dream world of novels, and fantasized about all she read, including the newspaper cuttings she sent Bywaters. Bywaters himself also dismissed the idea that Edith was trying to kill her husband. 'She had been reading books', he said. 'She had a vivid way of declaring herself. She would read a book and imagine herself as the character in the book'.

The extracts from the letters no doubt had a much greater impact on the judge and jury than perhaps they should have had. In the thousands of words of her outpourings, it is not surprising that some of her impassioned remarks were outrageous. Her counsel had another problem, too. Some extracts, such as 'I am still willing to dare all and risk all if you are' could as well apply to an abortion Edith was considering as to an intended murder. But of course in 1922 her counsel hesitated to explain this in her defence; the jury might well think that an admitted adulterer and abortionist could readily also be a murderer.

Edith Thompson claimed that all her stories were invented to bind Bywaters closer to her and keep his love. The judge was not impressed and his summing-up left little hope for either defendant. In two hours the jury found them both guilty and they were sentenced to hang. Edith protested: 'I am not guilty. Oh God, I am not guilty.'

There was a considerable public outcry about the proposed hanging of Edith Thompson. Thousands of signatures were collected in a petition for a reprieve. Three days before the execution date, Bywaters again attempted to save Edith, telling his mother: 'I swear she is completely innocent . . . she never knew about it . . . I can't believe they will hang her'.

This message was rushed to the Home Secretary, who had gone away for the weekend. It did no good. On 9 January 1923 Bywaters and Thompson were hanged at Pentonville and Holloway prisons respectively.

Edith Thompson was a silly woman who was carried away by love. But did she deserve to die? She became a cause célèbre, being the first woman hanged in Britain for 15 years. It was to be nearly 33 years before the last to be executed, Ruth Ellis, went to the gallows.

Below
The scene outside Holloway Prison on the morning of Edith Thompson's execution.

LIFE PLUS 99 YEARS

They had money, looks and brains, but sought their kicks in murder. The money bought the best lawyer....

Right
Robert Franks, the randomly chosen victim of the 'perfect' crime.

Crimes are committed for many reasons – greed, passion, lust, jealousy, even for fun – but it is rare that the most terrible crime of all, murder, is committed merely for kicks. In 1924, however, two extremely rich young men from Chicago shocked the world when they confessed to having killed an innocent boy only for the intellectual pleasure to be derived from committing 'the perfect crime'.

Nathan Leopold, 19, was the son of a millionaire. His IQ was at genius level, and he had graduated in philosophy at the University of Chicago. Richard Loeb was also at the university and was almost equally bright and equally rich, his father being vice-president of Sears Roebuck and Co, the giant mail order company. A year younger than Leopold, he was a local heart-throb.

Since the hardest crime to solve is the apparently motiveless one where criminal and victim are unknown to each other, the conspirators decided that the victim would be chosen by chance. A typewriter was stolen and a first ransom note was typed on it – a note informing the victim's father of a kidnapping and demanding $10,000 for the victim's return. The delivery of the money was to be arranged by telephone.

On 21 May 1924 the two drove off in search of their random victim. Robert Franks, 14, himself the son of a millionaire, was found where 49th Street met Ellis Avenue, and persuaded to get into the car. Leopold, by his account, was driving, and Loeb killed the boy in the car by hitting him on the head with a chisel. Leopold drove on to Hegewich, on the outskirts of Chicago, a place he knew because he used it for birdwatching.

The body was stripped, the face being made unrecognizable with hydrochloric acid, and then placed in a culvert, where the killers expected it would be washed away. The clothes and murder implement were either buried or burnt in the cellar of Loeb's house. The ransom letter, signed George Johnson, was then sent to the boy's

Nathan Leopold (left) and Richard Loeb in court as they are sentenced to life imprisonment.

father, Jacob Franks. Although the choice of victim was by chance it so happened that Franks and Loeb were distantly related.

The following day the car was cleaned of a little blood and Mr Franks was rung (Leopold did the talking) with ransom instructions. He was told to package up the money and go to a certain drugstore to pick up a letter which would tell him how the money was to be passed over. The letter instructed him to take a certain train, to watch for a landmark (a factory water-tower with a sign reading 'Champion'), to count five after passing it and then to throw the package as far as he could through the window.

However, whether this part of the 'perfect crime' would have worked or not and, if it had, whether its perpetrators would have dared to collect the money, is not

The drainpipe in which a workman discovered the body of Robert Franks.

known, for Mr Franks was dissuaded from carrying out the instructions by the discovery of the body that day by maintenance men and the announcement of this in the press.

The 'perfect crime' in fact was rapidly seen to be far from perfect. Spectacles found at the scene were traced to Leopold. They presumably fell from his jacket breast pocket when he was stooping with the body. The horn-rim frames were of a special type and had been supplied by a Chicago company to only three customers. Leopold was therefore rapidly traced and became an immediate suspect. He had not missed the spectacles, and at first when confronted with them did not think they belonged to him, but was unable to produce his own. He claimed that he must have lost them weeks earlier when bird-watching at the spot with Loeb and some girls.

Characteristics of the typed characters in the ransom notes were found to tally with those on documents typed at the university, showing that Leopold could have had access to the vanished machine. Under pressure Loeb broke down and confessed and, when confronted with his partner's confession, Leopold, too, confessed.

Their trial began on 2 July 1924 in the Criminal Court of Cook County. No expense was spared in their defence by their shocked families and Clarence Darrow, the most famous advocate in the United States, was engaged.

Darrow surprised everybody by persuading the defendants to plead guilty. This ruled out, at least in theory, a plea of insanity, which was generally assumed to be the only credible defence.

A plea of 'not guilty through insanity' meant a trial by jury, which Darrow considered would be biased in the climate of hatred which had built up against the defendants – hatred arising from the horror of the crime itself tinged with racism,

Clarence Darrow, whose eloquence saved Leopold and Loeb from execution.

the defendants being wealthy Jews. A 'guilty' verdict brought in by a jury would mean death by hanging. Darrow's plea meant that the judge alone would decide the fate of his charges.

Although the plea was 'guilty', the facts had to be established in court, and of course the important details of the crime were not in dispute. The crux came when Darrow, in presenting the case for the defence, based it on the idea of diminished responsibility due to the defendants' state of mind – in effect a plea of insanity 'through the back door'. The validity of this defence was vigorously contested by the prosecutor, Robert E. Crowe. After three days of argument, the judge ruled that it would be better for him to hear the evidence than to determine in advance what it might be.

Crowe had originally expected an insanity plea, so had lined up his psychiatrists in anticipation, and the court battle now became one between two groups of psychiatrists. Fundamentally, this was a battle that had been and would be waged hundreds of times in courts all over the world. The prosecution claimed that only if all perpetrators of such crimes were considered insane could the current defendants be considered so. The defence countered with the argument that the unhealthy, restricted childhood led by the two boys on account of the isolation resulting from their wealth, together with constitutional factors – in particular Leopold's abnormal intelligence and Loeb's tendency to fantasize his life in strange directions – inevitably inhibited a normal emotional growth.

Darrow, a master of oratory who was keenly opposed to capital punishment, made a brilliant 12-hour speech, in which he had the judge in tears. (It was a hallmark of his cases that jurors inevitably cried.) Crucial sentences can give a flavour:

> *'The easy thing and the popular thing to do is to hang my clients. I know it. Men and women who do not think will applaud. The cruel and thoughtless will approve ... I know the future is on my side. Your Honour stands between the past and the future. You may hang these boys; you may hang them by the neck until they are dead. But in doing it you will turn your face toward the past ... I am pleading for the future. I am pleading for a time when hatred and cruelty will not control the hearts of men, when we can learn by reason and judgement and understanding and faith that all life is worth saving and that mercy is the highest attribute of men.'*

Some impression of the power of Darrow's speech can be gained from Orson Welles' portrayal of the great advocate in

Nathan Leopold upon his release from prison in 1958.

the film *Compulsion*, from Ira Levin's novel based on the case.

Robert Crowe, the state attorney, while competent, could not match Darrow's eloquence, and in attempting to do so he annoyed the judge by suggesting that, so strong was his case, should the sentence not be death, there would be suspicions that the court had been bribed.

Judge Caverly sentenced Leopold and Loeb, chiefly on account of their youth, not to death but to life imprisonment, plus 99 years for kidnapping, with a recommendation that there should be no parole. Because of his 'leniency' he needed police protection after the trial. The case remained in the news for years, and the animosity towards the prisoners did not lessen – their birthdays were commemorated in the Chicago press in annual outbursts of hate. A similar unforgiving attitude on the part of the public was to be shown in Britain in the case of Brady and Hindley, who also murdered for thrills.

Richard Loeb became a homosexual in prison, and was murdered in January 1936, hacked to death in the bathrooms of Joliet State Prison by another prisoner, James Day, on whom he was trying to press a relationship. Nathan Leopold did his best to atone for his crime. He tried to help fellow-prisoners, ran the library, studied (he was said to have learned 37 languages) and volunteered for medical research in testing an anti-malaria drug. In 1949 Governor Adlai Stevenson commuted his 99-year sentence to 85 years, making him eligible for parole and, thanks to supporters such as Carl Sandburg, the poet, he was released on 13 March 1958, after serving $33\frac{1}{2}$ years of his sentence. He married and devoted himself to good work until his death following a heart attack on 30 August 1971.

HE REALLY DID DIE FOR HER

She bewitched a corset salesman, and together they battered her husband to death with a sash weight.

Judd Gray was an inoffensive 32-year-old salesman for the Bien Jolie Corset Company. If Gray was quiet, his wife, Isobel, was even quieter. A stay-at-home girl with few apparent interests other than keeping a tidy house, she seemed to derive her main pleasure from playing bridge with friends and occasionally dancing. Nothing much disturbed the even tenor of their innocent lives.

Judd's appearance seemed to fit his lifestyle. Slight, with circular wire-rimmed spectacles and constantly blinking eyes, he gave the impression of a studious man – far removed from the popular image of a commercial traveller in ladies' underwear. Indeed Judd could hardly bring himself to mention corsets – his word was 'corselets'.

It was surprising, then, in June 1925 to find Judd keeping a blind date with a 30-year-old married woman. She was Ruth May Snyder, of Scandinavian descent, and the two met with mutual friends in a booth in a New York eaterie – Henry's Swedish Restaurant. It was the time of Prohibition, and they drank bootleg gin and ate smorgasbord as they got to know each other.

If the phrase 'the attraction of opposites' has any meaning, it applied to Judd and Ruth. For if he was retiring, she was a sturdy woman with strong features and blond hair who confidently paraded her buxom charms, wearing a grey fox fur and noisy copper adornments. Her home life, too, seemed different from Judd's as she told him of a husband 13 years her senior, who had wedded her, aged 19 and an innocent. Ever since she had regretted her marriage to Albert Snyder, the art editor of a boating magazine, who, she claimed, had always despised her, their matrimonial life alternating between fighting and sullen silences.

Judd was captivated, and hours passed as the two compared their matrimonial problems – Judd confessing to an overwhelming (and, possibly, newly realized) boredom.

Judd Gray, seen here with his mother.

In August, after Ruth, her husband and their seven-year-old daughter Lorraine had been on holiday, she and Judd met again at Henry's, and Judd later took Ruth back to his empty office to get some camphor oil for her sunburnt shoulders. He dabbed it on to their mutual pleasure. Soon he was fitting her with a new 'corselet' and their liaison began.

Carried on in New York hotel bedrooms, the affair was dominated by Ruth, who made the obsessed Judd caress her feet. He would be her slave and would sink to his knees and call her 'Momsie'; and she would command him and call him 'Lover Boy'.

Soon Ruth told Judd of numerous 'accidents' that were befalling her husband. On one occasion she had given him a whisky while he worked on the engine of his car in the garage, after which he had felt drowsy but had noticed just in time that the garage doors had mysteriously shut and that he was breathing carbon monoxide.

A horrified Judd captured Ruth's drift, and she told him about the $96,000 insurance on her husband's life. After more amazing accidents had failed to finish off Albert Snyder, Ruth insisted that Judd should help her to get rid of her husband so that they could live rich and happy lives together. Refusal meant the withdrawal of her favours, and a besotted Judd agreed.

Judd was instructed to buy chloroform, a heavy sash weight and some wire for hanging pictures. One night he went round to the Snyders' clapboard house in Queens, New York, and familiarized himself with the layout. Ruth's husband and daughter were away, and the pair made passionate drunken love in the daughter's room.

On the night of Saturday/Sunday, 20 March 1926, Judd let himself into the Snyder house while the family was at a bridge party, and hid in the spare bedroom. He took a blue handkerchief and an Italian newspaper to leave as false clues.

When the Snyders returned, Lorraine was put to bed and Albert sank into a drunken sleep. Ruth then joined Judd and together they returned, with their implements of death, to the master bedroom. Judd smashed the sash weight on to Snyder's head, but succeeded only in waking him, and the frightened man fought for his life. Another blow failed to do the trick and Snyder grabbed Judd's tie, causing him to drop the weight. 'For God's sake help, Momsie,' he cried.

Ruth picked up the weight and her blow

stilled her husband without killing him. So she stuffed cotton wool soaked with chloroform into his nostrils and mouth, tied his hands and feet and strangled him with the wire. In the botched murder Ruth was still the stronger.

The killers washed up, hid the sash weight and, because Ruth wouldn't trust Judd with it, also hid Ruth's jewellery. When they had scattered furniture to make the crime look like a robbery, Judd gagged and bound Ruth in the spare bedroom and left for his hotel in Syracuse, where on the Monday he intended to take up his salesman's round.

A tapping noise woke Lorraine in the morning. She discovered her mother, ran for the neighbours, and soon Ruth was telling the story of a foreign-looking prowler, feigning hysteria on being told her husband was dead.

However, on examining her, the doctor did not believe her story of a struggle, and neither did the police. The displacement of the furniture was not authentic and the jewellery was found under a mattress. A cancelled cheque for $200 made out to Judd aroused suspicion and, acting on a

Left
Ruth Snyder in court with her attorneys. (Inset) Her husband, Albert Snyder.
Below
A police officer with the sash weight and picture wire used in the murder of Albert Snyder.

hunch, the police told Ruth that Gray had confessed all. She immediately admitted that a plan to kill her husband had been concocted, but that she had tried to back out and that Judd had been the killer.

The sash weight, the jewellery and the insurance policies were found and Judd was brought back from Syracuse. He told the police the whole story, explaining the power that Ruth had over him and how he had killed for her.

The pair were found guilty and sentenced to die in the electric chair. The writer Damon Runyon covered the trial for the *New York American* and described the inert 'scared-rabbit little' Judd as 'soggy looking as a dummy in his loose-hanging clothes'. Judd did not even glance at Ruth during the trial, while she often looked daggers at him. 'Her eyes are blue-green and as chilly looking as an ice-cream cone'.

Such was the fascination in Ruth that, in the hope of a reprieve, 164 men wrote during the trial offering her marriage. All wanted to be Momsie's new Lover Boy. They were disappointed. Ruth and Judd were executed within four minutes of each other in January 1928, Ruth first. Ruth made the headlines to the end. A camera was smuggled into the execution chamber by a photographer of the New York *Daily News* and a famous picture was published of the moment when the current was switched on and killed her.

LOUISVILLE, KY.
CORONET DRY GIN
RYE
RYE
EBONY SOAP
TALLS
OLD QUAKER
CAUTION
WHISKEY
MALT
WHISKEY
MILLS

The 1930s

A vampire, gangsters,
a kidnapping,
the best and worst of bank robbers,
and a case of
disputed identity.

Part of a haul of liquor and beer confiscated by police in Savannah, Georgia, during the Prohibition era, which ended in 1933.

THE VAMPIRE CAUGHT BY ACCIDENT

A glass of milk and a ham sandwich were to lead the king of monsters to the guillotine.

If the old master of suspense, Alfred Hitchcock, had made a film of the story of the 'Vampire of Düsseldorf', Peter Kürten, he would have had to tone down the vital encounter between Maria Budlick and Kürten which eventually led to his capture. The series of coincidences and accidents was too much. To appreciate them the scene must be set.

For four years from 1925 Düsseldorf had been a city in the grip of terror. It was clear that a maniac was at large. Police had marked to his credit 46 crimes of all kinds of violence and sexual perversion. It seemed that this man obtained most pleasure from attacking his victims with a variety of knives – but he was also known to use blunt instruments and his hands. Women were frequently sexually assaulted, but men and animals were also his prey. Four people had been killed, and many others severely injured, but one of the worst horrors was that he seemed to enjoy drinking his victims' blood – hence the name 'Vampire'.

In 1929 his rate of activity was increasing. The citizens of Düsseldorf were shocked when, on 23 August, two stepsisters, Luise Lenzen and Gertrud Hamacher, aged 14 and 5 respectively, were murdered when walking home across allotments from the annual fair at Flehe.

Right and opposite **Police photographs of Peter Kürten, the 'Vampire of Düsseldorf'.**

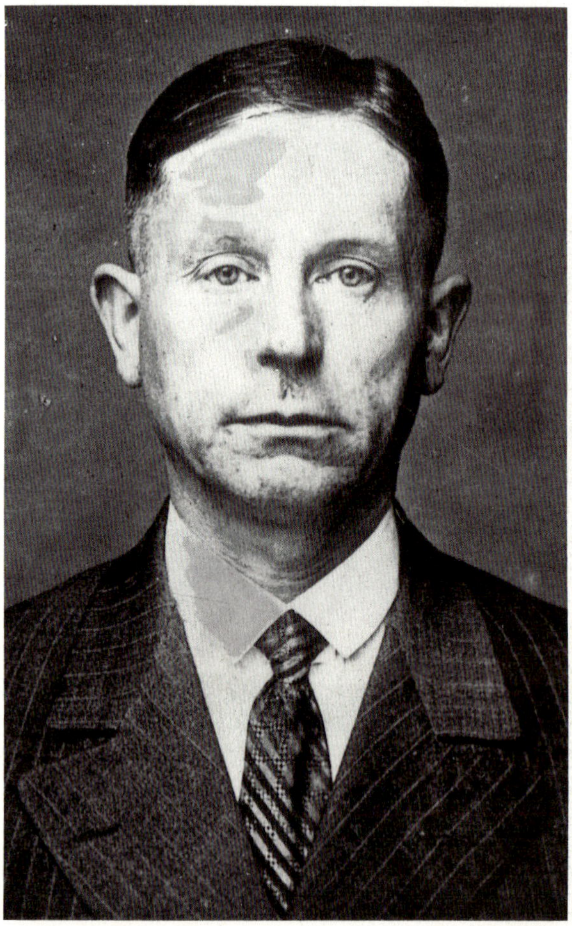

Both were strangled before their throats were cut.

Twelve hours later, 26-year-old Gertrud Schulte accepted an invitation to be taken to another fair by a man who, on reaching some woods, attempted to rape her. As she fought him off with the words 'I'd sooner die', she heard him reply 'Well, die then', stabbing her repeatedly with a knife. It broke as he threw her to the ground and half of it remained sticking in her back. Luckily her screams were heard. An ambulance and police were called and her life was saved. But the attacker had vanished.

The frenzy of his attacks continued to mount. A girl of 18, a man of 30 and a woman of 37 were all wounded within a single half-hour. Then two servant girls, Ida Reuter and Elisabeth Dorrier, were bludgeoned to death. In November a thin-bladed knife was the instrument of death: five-year-old Gertrud Albermann was slashed 36 times during her murder.

The Vampire was national news in Germany, of course, and he kept his name in the newspapers with a series of vicious attacks throughout the winter.

It is here that Maria Budlick enters the story. A 21-year-old maid, she lost her job in Cologne and on 14 May 1930 took the train to Düsseldorf, 30 kilometres away, to find new employment. She was well aware of the Vampire and determined to be careful.

Imagine, then, how our hypothetical film-maker would have directed the scene when she arrived at Düsseldorf, and was met off the platform by a man who offered to show her the way to a hostel. The tension would build up as she accepts and walks, unsuspectingly, through the town with him until he turns into Volksgarten

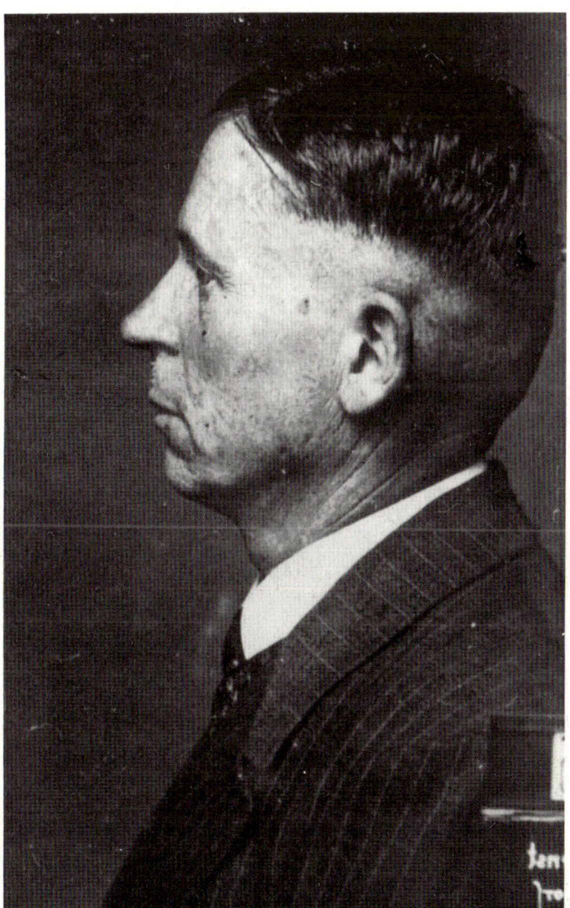

Above
Frau Meurer, one of the few women to survive an attack by Peter Kürten.

Right
Maria Hahn was one of many victims.
Below
The five-year-old Gertrud Albermann was repeatedly slashed in the course of her brutal murder.

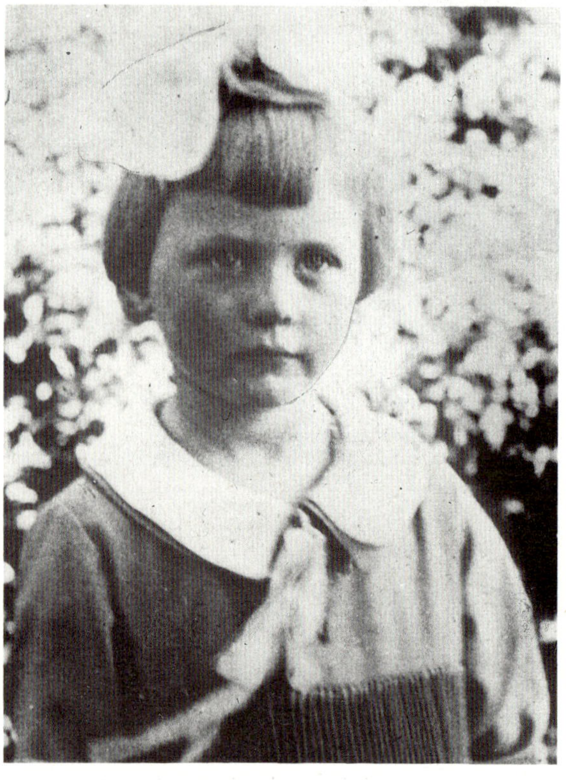

Park with its dark trees. At last she realizes her danger and tries to turn back, but the man argues and is insistent. Then, another man, quietly spoken, emerges from the shadows and asks if he can help. The first man withdraws, and the gallant knight escorts her away . . . to his home for a meal. A glass of milk and a ham sandwich later and he is taking her by tram to her hostel. But how would our film-maker then handle the short cut through Grafenburg Woods? What threatening music would presage the moment when he took her throat and attempted to rape her against a tree? For, irony of ironies, it was the second man who was the Vampire!

Maria had no chance, but as she was about to pass out the man asked if she remembered where he lived, in case she needed help again. 'No,' she replied, whether by fortune or foresight. The man relented, led her from the woods and departed.

Maria did, in fact, remember the street in which the man lived, for its name, Mettmannerstrasse, had impressed her. Strangely, and here is another twist, she decided not to tell the police. Instead, she put the details in a letter to a girlfriend. Fate now takes a hand again, for she misdirected the letter and it was read by a stranger. The camera now moves in for a close-up shot of a woman reading a stranger's letter and realizing with horror the implications – she was reading an account of the Vampire's latest attempted rape.

The woman took the letter to the police, and soon Maria Budlick was showing plain-clothes detectives 71 Mettmannerstrasse, where she had drunk milk and eaten with Kürten.

There was one more opportunity for our film director to build up the suspense. For Maria Budlick, entering the premises, caught sight of Kürten coming down the stairs. She rushed to tell her escort, following at a distance, but Kürten had seen her too, and he vanished.

His time at liberty was now short, however, and he knew it. He met his wife at the restaurant where she used to work until late at night and confessed to her that he was the Vampire of Düsseldorf. She was a former prostitute whom he had forced into marriage, but his relations with her had been normal. The last service she could do for him was to tell his story to the police. She told them where she would be meeting him next day, and armed police also kept the tryst. 'Don't worry,' he smiled as they

Maria Lappe, murdered in 1928.

surrounded him. 'There is no need to be afraid.'

Peter Kürten was a soft-spoken, mild man, whom his acquaintances could hardly believe was the Vampire. But at his trial, at a Düsseldorf drill-hall in April 1931, he confessed to a catalogue of 68 crimes, all of which he remembered in clear detail. He gave evidence from a tall cage and, in a matter-of-fact voice, told the story of his life. Well-dressed and groomed, he looked like a bank clerk, which made the story he told all the more horrifying for those who heard it.

One of a family of 13 whose brutish, drunken and unbalanced father would force himself on the mother in front of the children, he grew up in an atmosphere of incest, for which his father was imprisoned after relations with Kürten's 13-year-old sister. Kürten was later on to follow suit. At nine, he was apprenticed to a dog-catcher who lived in the house, and this man initiated him into torturing animals. Kürten claimed to have drowned a friend with whom he was playing on a raft and, when another friend dived in to try to rescue the boy, he held him under, too, until he was dead.

As his sexuality developed he began committing bestiality with sheep and goats, and obtained further orgasms from

Above
Rosa Ohliger, who was eight years old when she was murdered.
Above right
Ida Reuter, who was killed with blows from a hammer.

the blood which flowed when he stabbed them. He began living with a masochistic prostitute who taught him to abuse her. He turned to thieving and was imprisoned for two years, during which time his fantasies became more and more warped. On his release he attacked a girl during intercourse in the same Grafenburg Woods to which he was later to take Maria Budlick, and left her for dead, but she must have survived and not reported the incident. However, he was convicted for other assaults, but further long prison sentences only fed a grudge against society and fuelled his vicious fantasies further. He dreamed of poisoning schools full of children and on his release enjoyed indulging in arson, returning to the scene of the fires to enjoy the despair of the victims.

In 1913 Kürten carried out his first known murder, the victim being Gertrud Klein, a 13-year-old he came across asleep in a room he was burgling. He strangled her and cut her throat, and returned next day to enjoy the neighbours' horror. A curious aside is that he had wiped the blood on to his initialled handkerchief and then lost it at the scene. The girl's grandfather, Peter Klein, who had the same initials, was charged with the murder. He was acquitted through lack of evidence, but never recovered from the ordeal.

Kürten described the deaths of the girls from the fair: how he had sent the elder back for cigarettes while he killed the younger, and how he had repeated the performance when the elder returned. He described the pleasure he began to take from drinking the blood of his victims and how he enjoyed cutting the head off a swan in the park and putting the neck in his mouth.

Kürten was charged with nine murders and seven attempted murders, but the charges were academic as his full story unfolded and additional crimes were admitted. His own counsel claimed he was the king of sexual perverts, who killed anything he fancied – men, women, children or animals.

And yet the 48-year-old Kürten was quite sane, a clever man and, according to one medical witness, quite a nice one. The judge treated him sympathetically, drawing out the facts, but even he had had enough at the end, when Kürten began explaining that some of his victims had made things easy for him, and began moralizing on the man-hunting habits of modern women. The judge cut him short and later the jury took only $1\frac{1}{2}$ hours to find him guilty on all counts.

Kürten faced the guillotine on 2 July 1931. Even then he remained the complete criminal deviant. He wanted to know if, when his head was chopped off, he would still be able to hear for a moment the blood gushing from the stump of his neck, as it had from the neck of the swan in the park. 'That would be a pleasure to end all pleasures', said the Vampire of Düsseldorf.

Frau Meiner, one of the unfortunate nine with whose murders Kürten was charged.

THE BOSS OF THE CHICAGO UNDERWORLD

If Scarface hadn't existed, Hollywood would have had to invent him. Capone was larger than life, and larger than the movies.

Al Capone in court with his lawyers while facing charges of income tax evasion.

Al Capone had two serious convictions. He received a year in prison for carrying a gun without a permit – this he organized himself, the spell inside being a 'rest'. His other conviction was for tax evasion, for which he was sentenced to 11 years and served eight. This is hardly the record of a super-criminal. But Al Capone became the most famous of all gangsters, forever associated with the 'golden age' of hoodlums, the era of Prohibition in the 1920s.

Alphonse Capone was born in the slums of Brooklyn in 1899, the son of a Neapolitan barber. He was a petty criminal before joining the notorious Five Points Gang.

Capone's career was shaped by events in 1920. In January the Volstead Act came into effect prohibiting the sale of liquor in the United States. A man who saw the possibilities in marketing bootleg (illegal) liquor was a former New York gangster, Johnny Torrio, who was then operating in Chicago for his uncle, 'Big Jim' Colosimo, running the taverns and brothels. Torrio had earlier in Brooklyn been impressed by the fat, flashy but rough Capone and sent for him to be his bodyguard and right-hand man. Capone, already under investigation as a murder suspect, decided to join Torrio. Five months after the Volstead Act became law, Colosimo was murdered in his restaurant. Capone was spotted departing from the scene, but no charge was ever brought against him. Torrio inherited the empire he and his uncle had created and soon he and Capone were making millions of dollars a year running all Chicago's south-side crime. Cicero, which although a Chicago suburb was also the fifth largest city in Illinois, was 'owned' by the pair, who had their own politicians in power. Torrio was

still the boss of the outfit, with an estimated 700 hoodlums at his command.

By 1924 Capone, while still fat and carrying a scar on his face from early gang warfare (he was known as 'Scarface'), had become a smooth, well-dressed, bejewelled gangster chief with his own bodyguards. He operated illegal gambling, ran prostitution, owned nearly 200 bars and sold bootleg liquor, and he and Torrio were each making over $100,000 per week. But they did not have organized Chicago

The bloody aftermath of the St Valentine's Day Massacre.

crime to themselves. Their main rival was Dion O'Bannion, a gang chief whose cover was his florist's shop in North State Street.

In May 1924 O'Bannion sold a brewery to Torrio for $500,000, and then arranged for police to mount a raid while Torrio was inspecting it. Torrio was arrested and the brewery closed. This event led to a period of intense gang warfare in Chicago, resulting in over 1,000 deaths.

In November Mike Merlo, president of the Unione Siciliana, which made most of the illicit liquor and was under Torrio's protection, died, and $100,000 worth of flowers were sent to his funeral, many of them ordered from O'Bannion. On the day of the funeral three of Capone's men went to the shop ostensibly to purchase a floral tribute. O'Bannion, who carried three guns, held out his hand in greeting and,

while it was being shaken by one man, the other two shot him.

O'Bannion's funeral set the standard for the lavish gangsterdom funerals of the era. His corpse was laid out guarded by silver angels holding golden candlesticks. His airtight coffin, with silver and bronze walls and white satin couch, had a special tufted cushion for his hand to rest on, and there were 26 truckloads of flowers. A basket of roses was labelled: 'From Al'.

Johnny Torrio, who retired after narrowly escaping death, bequeathing his underworld empire to Capone.

Capone's power at this time was forcefully displayed by the murder of the bootlegger 'Ragtime Joe' Howard, who had manhandled Capone's bookkeeper. Capone walked up to Howard in a bar, emptied six shots into his head and departed. Although a dozen witnesses were present, none would dare testify against Capone, the inquest verdict being 'killed by parties unknown'.

Two months later Capone himself narrowly escaped death when three of O'Bannion's men riddled his car with machine-gun bullets. Capone had stepped out a minute earlier to inspect one of his restaurants. Next week, however, Johnny Torrio was gunned down by the same three men as he returned home with his wife from shopping. He survived with five bullet wounds only because Bugs Moran's gun jammed as he held it to the fallen Torrio's head for the coup de grâce. Guarded by Capone's gunmen while spending 16 days in hospital, Torrio then went to jail for his own safety. There he formally retired from bootlegging, handing his $50 million-a-year operation over to the 25-year-old Capone. Thus Capone, whose 'skills' did not lie in the patient building of an empire, inherited one of the most powerful in gangsterdom.

Capone still liked to deal personally with some of his problems. In 1925 he machine-gunned from a speeding car the assistant state attorney of Chicago – a popular method of execution in gangland. Although there were witnesses he was not charged. He was however charged three months later with the murder of a rival gangster, but was held for only one hour. In September he escaped death again when Earl 'Hymie' Weiss and Bugs Moran, who had taken over the O'Bannion gang, led eight carloads of gangsters to his Cicero headquarters, the Hawthorn Hotel, and methodically sprayed the building with over 1,000 rounds of machine-gun ammunition. Capone lay on the restaurant floor with his bodyguards around and on top of him, prepared to stop any bullets.

Three weeks later 'Hymie' Weiss was killed by Capone's men who took over rooms opposite his apartment and installed two machine-gun posts in them. He was shot after getting out of his car. A henchman was also killed, and three others, including his lawyer, were seriously injured.

Capone almost had the last word in this feud with the famous St Valentine's Day Massacre in 1929. His men, some in police uniforms, went to a garage owned by the Moran mob and lined up the seven men inside facing a wall. They then sprayed them with machine-gun fire. Moran ecaped by arriving late. He saw what he thought was a police car outside and did not go in.

Capone was now all-powerful, his rackets bringing in over $6 million per week. He was a marked man, of course, and his car was a $20,000, seven-ton steel 'tank' with a gun turret, bullet-proof windows and combination locks, and he travelled in convoy with guards.

Three months after the St Valentine's Day Massacre, he held a lavish dinner in his hotel, and afterwards rose to name three present as traitors. Two had been trusted gunmen, who had helped eliminate Weiss. In a rage, Capone took a baseball bat from beneath his chair, and went round the table to batter out the brains of the three men, one at a time, while they sat there too frightened to move.

Dion O'Bannion, a rival to Capone, who was gunned down in his florist's shop.

The following week Capone went to Philadelphia and was arrested, probably by arrangement, for carrying a gun. He was given a year's imprisonment, but with a private suite, telephone and radio, his meals brought in and visitors allowed at any time, it was more like a holiday. In fact while there he also had his tonsils removed and a nose operation, making use of his time while things cooled down. In his absence, however, Eliot Ness, a famous Prohibition agent, led a drive against his bootleg premises, closing many after emptying stocks and destroying equipment.

Capone described his bootlegging operation with unanswerable accuracy: 'When I sell liquor, it's bootlegging. When my patrons serve it on silver trays on Lake Shore Drive it's hospitality'. Soon after his release from prison he pleaded guilty to tax evasion, with an equally down-to-earth justification: 'I didn't know you paid taxes on illegal earnings'. He expected a short sentence, but for once his bribery did not work on officials, and a 'fixed' jury was replaced at the last minute. He was sen-

tenced to 11 years and was sent to Atlanta Penitentiary.

While in prison Capone began suffering from the effects of syphilis contracted years before. It took the form of paresis, a brain-wasting disease, and he rapidly degenerated into a rambling and raving lunatic. On 6 November 1939 he was released from Alcatraz and returned to his luxurious mansion at Palm Island, Florida. Former associates who visited him were heard to say he was 'as nutty as a fruit cake', still thinking he was running his crime business.

On the day of his release his mentor, Johnny Torrio, was sentenced to 30 months for tax evasion, a remarkable coincidence. Two days later, Edward O'Hare, an undercover agent who had helped send Capone to prison, was shot dead while driving in Chicago – if this was coincidence, it, too, was remarkable.

Capone 'enjoyed' his freedom for eight years. The man who had ordered violent deaths for several hundred rivals, died in bed of a stroke brought on by paresis in 1947 at the age of 48. He was buried in Chicago, at Mount Oliver Cemetery.

Capone, accompanied by a U.S. marshal, on his way to a federal penitentiary.
Left
Bugs Moran, who narrowly escaped being killed in the St Valentine's Day Massacre.

THE LEGENDARY BONNIE AND CLYDE

They were pursued through five states as they lived and died by the gun.

Above left
Bonnie Parker poses aggressively, cigar in mouth.
Above right
Clyde Barrow with a collection of assorted weaponry.

Bonnie and Clyde are the subjects of a famous song, a film was made about them, and their exploits have acquired an aura of glamour. In fact, they were gangsters of limited intelligence whose career of robbery lasted a little more than two years. John Dillinger described them as 'punks who are giving bank robbers a bad name'.

Clyde Chestnut Barrow was born in Telice, Texas, on 24 March 1909, one of eight children. He was reputedly a cruel child and developed early his taste for cars and guns. He was only 17 when first caught stealing a car, an offence for which, as a first-time offender, he escaped punishment.

Bonnie Parker was a tiny, brassy blonde, some 20 months younger than Clyde. They met about January 1930 and were soon waging a war against the law, which ended only when Clyde was arrested and sentenced to 14 years' imprisonment on charges of car theft and burglary. Bonnie was a tough ex-waitress who had been disastrously married at 16 – her husband, Roy Thornton, had been sent to jail for murder. Although now hardly 19 she was already a cigar-smoking nymphomaniac to whom being a gangster's moll seemed an attractive way of life. She smuggled a gun to Clyde in prison and he escaped, but five days later was caught again in Middleton, Ohio, and sent back to Texas, where he was imprisoned in the state penitentiary at Huntsville.

Clyde persuaded a fellow prisoner to chop off two of his toes in an effort to escape the exhausting work of the chain gang, but it was a futile gesture, because on 2 February 1932 the governor of Texas, 'Ma' Ferguson, granted a general pardon, and Clyde was released, still on crutches.

By March Bonnie had left home to join Clyde, but there was to be a hitch before their life as gangsters on the road began, because she was detained by police over

The vicious pair in a playful mood.

the matter of a stolen car. Meanwhile, Clyde and some associates, notably Ray Hamilton, had begun murdering in the course of their robberies – a jeweller was killed in Hillsboro, Texas, and in Atoka, Oklahoma, two lawmen who recognized them outside a barn dance hall, Sheriff C. G. Maxwell and his deputy, Eugene Moore, were shot dead.

Bonnie eventually caught up with Clyde and Hamilton, and they were also joined for a time by Clyde's brother Buck, who had escaped from Eastham Prison, Texas. The proceeds of their robberies were not large – $3,500 was considered such a coup that they decided to visit Hamilton's father

Right
Bonnie Parker with her mother, to whom she was deeply attached.

in Michigan, but Hamilton got drunk, was arrested, and was sent back to Texas, where he was sentenced to 263 years for his part in the robberies and murder.

Bonnie was a very active partner in the gang, and it was she who allegedly shot a butcher three times in the stomach during a robbery. They had now been joined by the 16-year-old William Daniel Jones, who hero-worshipped Clyde. Quite how far Bonnie spread her sexual favours around the gang is not recorded, but Clyde was known to have homosexual tendencies (he was not impotent as suggested in the film) and Bonnie an intense sexual appetite, so no doubt Jones was a useful substitute for Hamilton.

Successful bank robberies were carried out at Abilene, Texas, and Orenogo, Missouri, but in December 1932 a man was killed when they stole a car.

At the very beginning of 1933 Bonnie, Clyde and Jones escaped a police trap set up in Dallas, killing Deputy Sheriff Malcolm Davis in their escape. They were now notorious and decided to lie low in an apartment in Joplin, Missouri, where they were rejoined by Clyde's brother Buck, who brought his wife, Blanche. A suspicious neighbour informed the police and another trap was set, from which the gang escaped by crashing through a garage door and hitting police cars blocking the way. Clyde and Jones acquired minor wounds, but two policemen were shot dead and another was badly injured.

Their bank-robbing career continued but now everybody was looking for them and increasingly they were forced to sleep in the cars they stole. Then Bonnie, Clyde and Jones crashed their car into a gorge after a bridge had collapsed. Bonnie was badly burned. They were looked after by a farmer, but he guessed who they were and they were soon on the run again.

Luckily for them, a doctor at Fort Smith, Arkansas, was persuaded to treat Bonnie, who should have been in hospital. Buck and Blanche joined them again, and in June 1933 the gang robbed a bank in Alma, and a Piggly-Wiggly store in Fayetteville, Texas, where they shot dead the new marshal, Henry Humphrey, who had

chased them. His death followed a raid which netted only $50.

In Iowa filling stations were robbed for small amounts, and at Platte City, Missouri, they ran into another police ambush. Buck was hit and terribly wounded in the head and Blanche injured by glass, but they escaped again and holed up in picnic grounds by a river at Dexter, Ohio.

With Buck, Bonnie and Blanche all badly hurt, it was impossible now to avoid detection. On 24 July 200 police surrounded them and there followed a three-hour

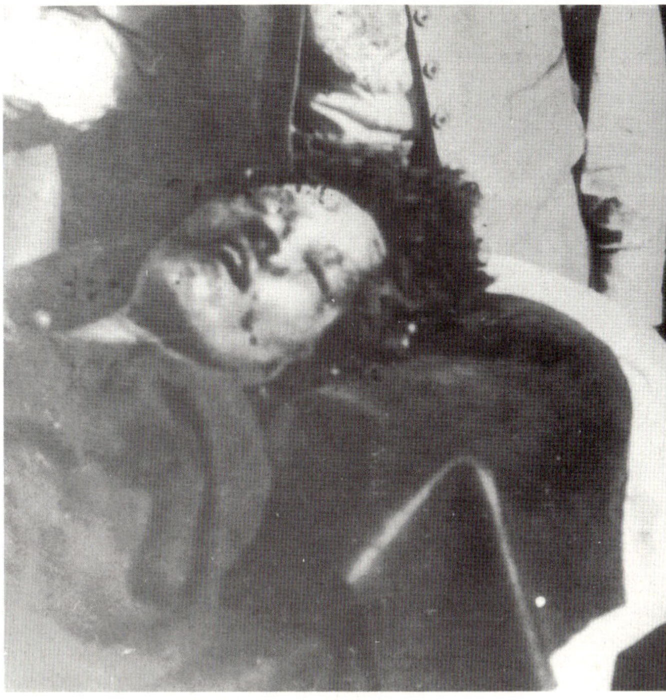

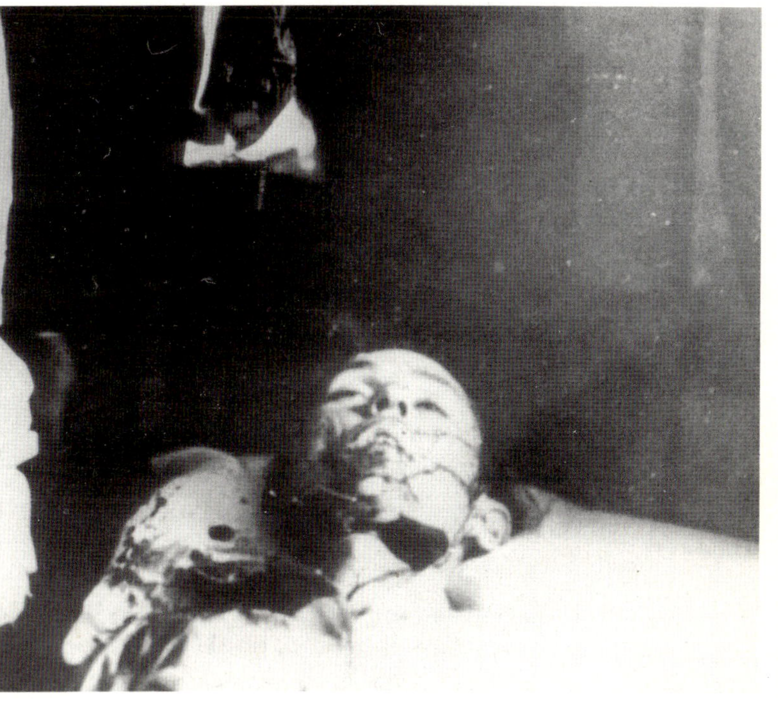

gun battle. Buck was hit three more times, in hip, shoulder and back, and was obviously going to die. Blanche stayed with him and police found them together but, incredibly, Bonnie, Clyde and Jones got across the river and escaped in another car. All were wounded. Buck was to live for six days; Blanche received a ten-year prison sentence.

The others managed to lie low until their wounds healed, when Jones finally left Bonnie and Clyde to themselves. Clyde dressed in a blond wig and women's clothes to avoid being spotted, and by the end of 1933 the pair were once more existing on the proceeds of small robberies. They returned to Dallas, but were nearly caught at Grand Prairie, Texas.

In January 1934 their old ally, Ray Hamilton, escaped from prison with other former associates Joe Palmer and Henry Methvin, and the fugitives once more had occasional companions during their exploits. With Methvin, they were interrupted at a picnic with Bonnie's family at Grapevine, near Dallas, by two highway patrolmen and shot them both dead. Five days later they killed another inquisitive policeman near Miami.

Bonnie and Clyde's downfall was to be at the hands of a betrayer – either Methvin or his father seeking a deal with the police. A Texas ranger, Frank Hamer, and five of his men waited in bushes by the roadside eight miles from Gibsland, Louisiana, having been tipped off that Bonnie and Clyde would be driving past. At 9 am on 23 May 1934 the bandits' car appeared and the officers raked it with hundreds of bullets from machine-guns and rifles. Dozens found their mark and Clyde, driving without shoes, and Bonnie, halfway through a sandwich, were killed almost instantly.

Their numerous shoot-outs had made them legends, and thousands flocked to their funerals. But in reality, aged only 25 and 23, they were pathetic figures and their two years together on the run had been a sordid episode of appalling violence for meagre rewards.

Above left
The bullet-shattered bodies on display after the police shootout.
Below left
The Texas Rangers who ambushed Bonnie and Clyde.

PUBLIC ENEMY NUMBER ONE

The dashing robber took his girlfriend to the movies, but he was betrayed and the last reel was his own ambush.

John Dillinger displaying his armoury.

A former German army officer, Herman K. Lamm, perfected a system of robbing banks which made his gang wealthy in the America of the 1920s. Each member of the gang had his job (lookout, guard, driver, etc.) and the operation was timed by the guard at the door with a stopwatch.

However, on 16 December 1930 an amazing chapter of accidents led to the gang's demise. The getaway Buick used for a robbery at Clinton, Indiana, burst a tyre on a kerb as they pulled away and the replacement vehicle grabbed by the gang was fitted with a governor preventing it from doing more than 35 mph. After a time this car was abandoned in favour of a truck, but this soon broke down, so they commandeered another car. This turned out to contain only one gallon of petrol and just failed to reach the border of Illinois. By now the authorities had caught up and the gang decided to shoot it out with their pursuers. After a long siege most were dead, but two surrendered with empty guns: James 'Oklahoma Jack' Clark and Walter Dietrich. They were sentenced to imprisonment, Dietrich serving his sentence at Michigan City prison, Indiana, where he met John Herbert Dillinger.

That Dillinger was in prison at all this time was an injustice. Born in Indianapolis on 22 June 1903, the son of a Quaker who owned a grocery store, he had had an unhappy childhood under strict religious parents. As a young man he had joined the US Navy but had deserted. In 1923 he had stolen a car for a joyride and got away with it, but the following year he was caught when, with a partner, he attempted to rob a grocer in Martinsville, Indiana. His father had persuaded him to plead guilty – it was a first offence and a lenient sentence could be expected. Instead, Judge Joseph Williams, who belonged to the same masonic lodge as the grocer, had awarded him concurrent sentences of two to 14 years for attempted robbery and ten to 20 years for conspiracy to commit a felony. A later governor of Indiana was to say that 'this obvious injustice had much to do with the bitterness which ... made Dillinger what he was'.

Little Bohemia Lodge, Wisconsin, where Dillinger escaped from a police ambush.

Another thing which made Dillinger what he was – 'Public Enemy Number One' – was the tuition he received in Michigan City prison from Walter Dietrich. The sophisticated system of robbing banks thought out by Lamm was passed on to Dillinger, and when he was paroled in 1933 he made full use of it. Dillinger was released on parole after hundreds of people from his home town of Mooresville had signed a petition (including the grocer who had been his victim). 'They stole nine years of my life,' said Dillinger, 'and now I'm going to do some stealing in return.'

Three weeks or so after he left prison the National Bank of New Carlisle, Indiana, was relieved of $10,600, and a week later the Commercial Bank in nearby Daleville made an involuntary contribution of $3,500. Over the next three months several banks were successfully robbed and Dillinger established a reputation. A smart dresser, he behaved with politeness and conducted his affairs like a film-star, resembling in particular the dashing Douglas Fairbanks Snr. Dillinger would nonchalantly vault the six-foot cages erected on some bank counters with the athleticism with which Fairbanks would scale balconies in romantic silent films. Dillinger would also raise his straw hat to the bank tellers – a very elegant gangster.

On 22 September 1933 Dillinger was arrested at the apartment of his girlfriend, Mary Longnaker, at Dayton, Ohio, and held at Lima, Ohio, to await trial. Four days later there was a big breakout from the Michigan City prison. Dillinger had earlier managed to smuggle guns into the prison, and ten bank robbers used them to escape. Among them were James 'Oklahoma Jack' Clark and Walter Dietrich, Dillinger's mentors.

The first task of the escapees was, naturally, to rob a bank, the second to try to release Dillinger. The first proved easy. To accomplish the second three bandits went to Lima posing as officers from Indiana who wanted to question Dillinger. When Sheriff Jess Sarber asked to see credentials, he was shown a gun, and when he resisted he was shot. Dillinger, released, asked his rescuers: 'Did you have to do that?' when he saw Sarber dying.

Dillinger now had a powerful and ruthless gang. They visited a police arsenal

Below
Evelyn 'Billie' Frechette, one of Dillinger's girl friends, seen here with her attorney.

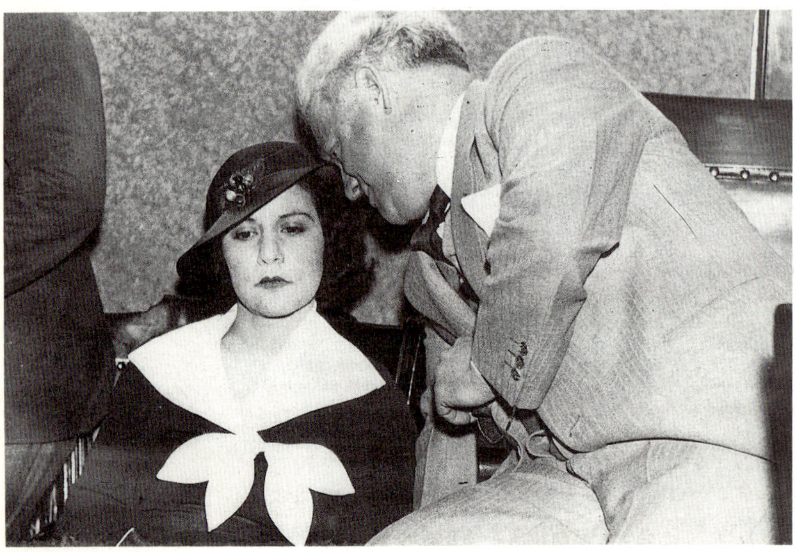

pretending to be reporters wanting to see the weapons to be used against 'the Dillinger gang'. The gullible overseer soon found a gun that wasn't his pointing at him – and promptly lost a supply of sophisticated weapons and ammunition. Four days later the Central National Bank of Greenside handed over $75,346 to a gang well-schooled in the carefully timed technique devised by Herman Lamm. A customer was politely allowed to keep his own money by Dillinger, who was maintaining his smooth image and emphasizing that his grudge was against society as a whole, not individuals.

Dillinger after his recapture in Tucson, Arizona, and return to jail.

In November 1933 Dillinger, out driving with another girlfriend, Evelyn 'Billie' Frechette, was spotted by detectives who gave chase, shooting at the couple, but Dillinger's car was powerful enough to enable him to get away. Five days later Dillinger and partners helped themselves to over $20,000 from a bank at Racine, Wisconsin.

Dillinger was captured again while on holiday with three of his gang in Tucson, Arizona. His three associates were taken to Ohio, to face charges of murdering Sheriff Sarber of Lima. Dillinger was taken to Indiana and charged with murdering a policeman at a bank robbery in Chicago, a crime which, it is generally conceded, he did not commit.

Dillinger, an escape artist, was held with maximum security: six doors and about 50 guards were considered sufficient to make the jail escape-proof. In the event they were not – in six weeks he was free. According to legend, he carved a very realistic gun from the rim of a washboard and blackened it with boot polish. It was enough to fool a guard and get him out of jail. (It is believed he actually had a real gun, smuggled in by a judge for a big payoff.) Dillinger took Herbert Youngblood, a murderer, and two machine-guns with him. He used the sheriff's fast car to escape to Illinois – and thus committed his first federal offence, that of stealing a car and taking it over the state line. The FBI were now involved in the attempt to catch Dillinger, who was fast becoming a popular figure, acquiring additional glamour when the FBI named him 'Public Enemy Number One'.

Ten days later Dillinger was injured in the arm when a policeman fired at the gang taking $52,000 from a bank in Iowa. A partner, John Hamilton, was more seriously injured in the shoulder and died.

In April 1934 FBI agent Melvin Purvis, on information received, had Dillinger and his gang trapped in Little Bohemia Lodge at Manitowish Waters, Wisconsin, but the operation was bungled. The wrong car was fired on by the agents and three innocent people were hit (one was killed), while the gang escaped from the back. An FBI agent was killed by the notorious 'Baby Face' Nelson, who had joined the gang. 'Billie' Frechette was captured during the raid and was to get two years' imprisonment for harbouring Dillinger.

The FBI was the target of considerable criticism as a result of this episode, and the press and public seemed more sympathetic to the cavalier Dillinger than to the agents of law and order. Dillinger had consistently claimed that killing was for hoods and hoodlums, and that he had no need or wish to kill anybody.

On 22 July 1934, a stifling hot Sunday, another FBI agent, Sam Cowley, received

The Biograph Theater, Chicago, outside which Dillinger was shot dead by federal agents.

a call from Anna Sage, a Chicago brothel-keeper. She told Cowley that she and Dillinger, and Dillinger's new girlfriend, Polly Hamilton Keele, were leaving for the cinema. She was betraying him for the reward. To help them spot Dillinger easily in the crowd, she would wear a bright orange-red skirt.

Thus it was that armed members of the 40-strong FBI 'Dillinger squad' watched the party enter the Biograph Theater to see Clark Gable play a stylish criminal, rather like Dillinger, in *Manhattan Melodrama*. Two hours later they were waiting in strategic positions when the audience emerged after the show. Dillinger, in dark glasses, straw hat and neat shirt and trousers, was soon surrounded by agents under the command of Melvin Purvis, and when he reached for his gun he was promptly shot dead.

The press and public were not overjoyed at this outcome. Passers-by had again been put in great danger and a woman received a bullet in the knee. The *New York Times* pointed out that driving a stolen car over a state line seldom incurs the penalty of being shot on the spot.

But was Dillinger shot? It is known that a lawyer, Louis Piquett, had just arranged painful face and finger surgery for him, the first as disguise, the second to destroy his fingerprints. Jay Robert Nash, author of *The Dillinger Dossier* and other books on crime, has claimed that Melvin Purvis was duped by Piquett and the corrupt East Chicago Police Department over the whole Biograph Theater affair, and that the man shot was one James Lawrence. Dillinger, thinks Nash, went to Oregon with his ill-gotten gains and was still alive in North Carolina in 1972.

THE PYJAMA GIRL

'Who was the murderer?' became secondary to 'Who was the corpse?' in a ten-year Australian mix-up.

When a murder is committed there is often considerable doubt as to the identity of the murderer and many murders remain unsolved. Sometimes it is impossible to identify the victim, in which case the murderer almost always goes free. But in one extraordinary case in Australia a body was preserved for ten years while its identity was argued about – there being two 'claimants'. And at the end, although a man was imprisoned for manslaughter, experts are still far from convinced about who it was who was killed.

The story starts on 1 September 1934 when the body in question was found by a farmer stuffed in a culvert by the side of a road near Albury, just on the New South Wales side of the border with Victoria. The body was that of a young woman dressed in her pyjamas who was to become famous as 'the Pyjama Girl'. She had a bag over her head and there were bad burns on one side of the body.

A post-mortem was performed in Albury and a bullet wound was found below the right eye. There were also three terrible wounds to the head, which had been caused by hard blows from a blunt instrument. Death had occurred up to about four days earlier. A further post-mortem in Sydney University confirmed that the woman had died from the gunshot wound, the head injuries, which would have killed her eventually, having been inflicted beforehand.

The pathologists built up a picture of the woman: 22–28 years old, Anglo-Saxon, blue-grey eyes, strangely shaped ears, small breasts, large hands and so on. The body was then preserved in a metal container filled with a solution of formaldehyde.

Linda Agostini, whose identification with the Pyjama Girl remains a subject of controversy.

A description and an impression of the girl's face were published in newspapers, with the result that a Mrs Presley went to the police and identified the body. It belonged, she said, to her granddaughter, born Anna Morgan, later Mrs Cootes, who had been living in a flat in Sydney. Others were brought in to see the body. John Morgan, Mrs Presley's first husband and the victim's grandfather, confirmed her story. A Mrs Callow, who had been Anna's landlady, also agreed that the body was hers.

However, one important person disagreed with this identification. Mrs Jeannette Routledge, Anna's mother, was con-

Antonio Agostini (left) was convicted of the manslaughter of his wife, Linda.

vinced that the body was not her daughter's. And thus confusion reigned, with nobody doing very much for four years, when a Sergeant King of the local police saw the corpse and claimed that it belonged to Linda Agostini, a woman whom he had known well until around 1931.

Linda Agostini, née Platt, was an English girl who had married Antonio Agostini, an immigrant Italian waiter, in 1930, a couple of years after Agostini had entered Australia and settled in Sydney. Linda Agostini, police discovered from a friend, had been alive in August 1934. However, Agostini himself claimed that he was separated from her by then – in fact he had reported her missing after she had left him for a lover. Moreover, he said the body was not that of his wife.

An inquest was belatedly held, and despite the disagreement of Sergeant King and Mrs Routledge, the coroner decided that the corpse was that of the former Anna Philomena Morgan and that she had been murdered by a person or persons unknown. There were now five witnesses to give positive identification.

Naturally the strange case of the four-year-old pickled corpse aroused public interest and Dr Palmer Benbow, a well-known amateur sleith, decided to try to find out what he could about the mysterious 'Pyjama Girl', whose presumed murder the police seemed to be having such singular lack of success in investigating.

As a medical man he found it easy enough to examine the body, but he also managed to study the pyjamas, the bag which covered the head and, inside the bag, a piece of towelling which contained laundry marks.

Much to the embarrassment of the police, Dr Benbow made very rapid progress. He came across a hut on common ground near Albury which contained a dilapidated old bed painted in a colour which matched specks of paint found on the body. He also discovered fibres which matched some found in the hair of the dead woman. The victim could have been murdered here – how had the police overlooked the old hut?

Even more to the point, Dr Benbow found an acquaintance of Anna Morgan who said that a man had beaten her up with a piece of the old bedstead. Here at least was apparently confirmation of the inquest verdict – the body was Anna Morgan's. But was the 'person unknown' of the verdict also coming to light? For this man told Dr Benbow who it was who had beaten Anna Morgan....

At this point Dr Benbow's investigations encountered strong disapproval on the part of the police and his further progress was obstructed. The man named, it seemed, was a close friend of a commissioner of police. The lawyers acting for Anna Morgan's mother, who knew of the doctor's enquiries, tried unsuccessfully to get the whole case reopened by the ruse of applying for Anna Morgan's estate.

Nothing happened now for another six

years, while the Pyjama Girl still lay in formaldehyde at Sydney University. Then, astonishingly, Antonio Agostini, now calling himself Tony, went to the commissioner and in a long statement confessed to the killing of his wife ten years previously. He said the couple had moved from Sydney to Melbourne in 1934 (Albury was between the two cities), but the marriage was going through a bad patch. One morning Agostini woke to find his wife holding a gun, the implication being she was either about to kill him or herself. He grabbed her, the gun went off, the bullet entered her cheek and killed her. In a panic he decided to get rid of the body but he dropped it at the top of the stairs – hence the head injuries. He then took the body by car to the culvert and tried to set fire to it.

Remarkably, in view of the fact that nothing much had happened for six years, it now took only days to find six people, in addition to Sergeant King, to identify the much-viewed body as that of Linda Agostini, and a second inquest was held.

Once more there were arguments about whether the body belonged to Linda Agostini or to Anna Morgan, and lawyers for the police, Agostini and Anna Morgan's mother were there to argue the case.

The heated disputes could hardly lead to anything conclusive at this late stage. There was the matter of the poor corpse's breasts, which were small and firm, as Anna's had been, whereas Linda's had been large and drooping. It was suggested and denied, that the formaldehyde had shrunk them (it had certainly shrunk the skin, and morticians had improved the appearance of the body for this new round of identifications). On the other hand, there was the question of the eyes. Anna's were blue-grey but those of the corpse were brown. An expert explained this was due to the 'pickling' process.(The original post-mortem had described the eyes as blue-grey.) There were also allegations that the teeth had been interfered with.

In the end, the coroner sided once again with the majority of the identification witnesses, and declared the body to be that of Linda Agostini. So the body had now been officially assigned to two different people. A minor mystery of the case was, of course, that it could belong to only one of them. What had happened to the other woman that she did not come forward while all this speculation was in the newspapers?

The way was now clear for Agostini to be convicted of manslaughter, and he received three years' imprisonment. This merely added another mystery to the whole affair, because his story was clearly not true, the head injuries being completely inconsistent with a dead body being dropped down the stairs as he claimed. After serving his sentence he was deported to Italy.

Before that the sadly ill-used corpse of the Pyjama Girl had at last been decently buried. Some people believe that the name under which it was buried, Linda Agostini, was but the final indignity that Anna Morgan suffered.

A STRANGE TRIANGLE OF PASSION AND DIGNITY

The besotted teenager killed out of jealousy, but his distraught mistress could not carry on living.

Alma Rattenbury with her husband and son, John.

Imagine an 'eternal triangle' in which the participants are of three generations. The case of Francis Rattenbury, aged 66, Mrs Alma Rattenbury, 37, and George Stoner, 17, was not the usual kind of triangle, but its salacious details provided the material for columns of newspaper reporting in the mid-1930s.

Francis Rattenbury was an architect, who had retired to the genteel south-coast town of Bournemouth, known for its respectability and, some would say, its dullness. His wife Alma was attractive and vital, and fancied herself as an artist. She had been married twice before and was described as a rather passionate woman, although no passion existed between herself and her rather boring husband. They slept on different floors at the Villa Madeira, their large house, and Francis

Rattenbury's last comforter each night was the whisky bottle.

The wealthy Rattenburys could afford a companion for Alma, a certain Irene Riggs. Their small son John completed the household until, in 1934, they advertised in the *Bournemouth Daily Echo* as follows: 'Willing lad wanted, aged 14–18, for housework. Scout training preferred'.

The lad who answered the advertisement and was duly appointed was George Stoner, who lived with his grandmother and had previously worked part-time at a garage.

Soon Alma Rattenbury was Stoner's mistress in more senses than one. The surprised lad found himself sharing her bed each night in this unconventional household. If Francis Rattenbury knew of the arrangement he seemed not to care, unconscious as he was at bedtime from the effects of whisky. Irene Riggs knew, and was shocked, but what concern of hers was it?

Alma Rattenbury was obsessed with her young lover, and Stoner found a completely new way of life – one he liked. He began strutting around like the master of the house whose position he had usurped. Less than six months after answering the advertisement, he was Mrs Rattenbury's companion for four days in the Kensington Park Hotel in London. With the £250 she had obtained from her husband, Alma took Stoner on a spending spree, buying him fashionable clothes and taking him to expensive restaurants. She bought a diamond ring for him to give to her, and at night he wooed her in his new crêpe-de-chine pyjamas. After this taste of the good life his behaviour back at the Villa Madeira became overbearing.

Strangely enough it was Stoner's jealousy which provoked the crisis in their lives. On their return Mrs Rattenbury found her husband depressed. She suggested that they spend a night with friends at Bridport and that Stoner should drive them there. The young buck realized that the Rattenburys would have to share a room and told Alma he would not take them, but she would not back down and went ahead with the arrangements.

George Stoner, Alma Rattenbury's young lover.

On 24 March 1935 Stoner went to his grandparents' house and borrowed a mallet 'to drive in some tent pegs'. At 10.30 that night Irene Riggs, on a trip from her bedroom to the lavatory, saw him peering over the banisters in his pyjamas, listening to the snores of Mr Rattenbury, who had fallen asleep with his whisky in a chair downstairs. A little later she was joined in her room as usual by Alma Rattenbury – the two normally had a night-time chat. Alma was excited about the visit to Bridport.

Fifteen minutes later, Irene Riggs was disturbed by Alma Rattenbury's scream from downstairs. Rushing down she saw Francis Rattenbury, in his armchair, his head smashed in and blood pouring out everywhere. She sent Stoner for the nearby Dr O'Donnell, who in turn sent for a surgeon, as Rattenbury was, miracu-

Right
Holiday visitors to Bournemouth sign a petition for George Stoner's reprieve.

lously, still alive. He was, however, to die four days later.

Alma Rattenbury seemed to go completely off her head that night, and began drinking heavily and blabbering on about her husband having read a book – she produced it – in which a man committed suicide, and saying that he admired this and that he himself had lived too long and would do the same (as if a man could smash in his own head).

When the police arrived Alma was gibbering mindlessly. She played records noisily, and made sexual advances to one of the policemen. She was immediately suspected of the crime, and produced a series of confessions. 'I did it with a mallet,' she wept.

Nearly two hours later Dr O'Donnell, a friend, returned, and complained to the inspector that Alma was suffering from the effects of shock, a large dose of morphia he had given her and the quantity of whisky she had taken.

However, in the morning Alma Rattenbury was charged with the attempted murder of her husband, a charge which became murder when Rattenbury died. When this occurred Stoner, who had remained silent and calm for four days, told Irene Riggs that he was responsible and would give himself up. She immediately told the police and Stoner, too, was charged.

Alma Rattenbury and George Stoner were impressive in their separate attempts to take the whole blame and thereby save the other. Stoner insisted he had seen Alma kiss her husband goodnight from the

The Villa Madeira, the Rattenbury's home, where husband and wife slept in different rooms.

French windows, and when Rattenbury was asleep had hit him and had then gone up to tell Alma. Stoner insisted he had not been influenced by Mrs Rattenbury, who had known nothing of his intentions.

Alma Rattenbury withdrew her confessions only at the trial, when her lawyers convinced her that they could not affect Stoner's case. She then related in a calm, frank manner how Stoner had come to her bed as usual that fatal night and told her he was in trouble. After some minutes' questioning he confessed that he had hit Rattenbury with a mallet which he had hidden in the garden. She had gone downstairs, had witnessed the scene and had tried to talk to her husband and revive him. She had screamed only when she had trodden on his false teeth and the full horror of the situation had struck her. She said she

Above
Alma Rattenbury, after her acquittal, in the company of her doctor.

began drinking whisky fast to save herself from being sick, but this had failed, so she had another, and then several more, and from then on could remember nothing.

Examination and cross-examination could not drag from Alma Rattenbury one memory of those grotesque hours in that room stained with blood when she had drunk, wept, confessed, babbled and continually played record after noisy record on her gramophone. Her mind was a complete blank.

She was impressive and dignified in the witness box and the jury believed her story. She was acquitted, and George Stoner was convicted and sentenced to death.

It had been a sensational trial and the press made the most of Alma Rattenbury's release. Little did the proprietors of the *Bournemouth Daily Echo* realize what big news would emerge from the small advertisement they had carried only months before.

But the final sensation had yet to come. Mrs Rattenbury could not live without George Stoner, who in the end had proved himself as gallant as the people to whose station in life he had so cruelly been taught to aspire. Three days after her release she neatly laid her fur coat and handbag on a river bank, enjoyed a last cigarette, and stabbed herself savagely six times in the breast with a knife. Three blows pierced her heart. A man watching her from afar saw her sink into the water and drift away. Thousands attended her funeral.

Ironically, George Stoner was reprieved and his sentence reduced to life imprisonment.

THE LINDBERGH BABY

Paying for gas with the wrong currency led to his trial for murder, but was the German carpenter framed?

Charles Lindbergh arriving in Croydon after his successful flight across the Atlantic.

There were few better-known men in the United States in 1932 than Colonel Charles A. Lindbergh, who had become famous in 1927 by making the first non-stop translatlantic flight in his aircraft *Spirit of St Louis*. The whole country was therefore shocked and saddened to hear that on 1 March his 19-month-old son, Charles A. Lindbergh, Junior, had been kidnapped.

The colonel, his wife Anne, whom he had met after a flight to Mexico City (she was the daughter of the US ambassador) and their nursemaid, Betty Gow, had been in their luxurious large new house at Hopewell, New Jersey, at the time of the kidnapping, which was discovered just after 10 pm. Beneath the nursery window were indistinct footprints, presumably made by a kidnapper who had removed his shoes. Nearby were a chisel and a roughly made ladder in three sections. The ladder was broken where the middle section fitted into the top part. On the nursery window sill was a badly written and misspelt note. It read:

Dear Sir, Have 50,000$ redy, 25,000$ in 20$ bills 15,000$ in 10$ bills and 10,000$ in 5$ bills. After 2–4 days we will inform you were to deliver the mony.
We warn you for making anyding public or for notify the police.
The child is in gut care.
Instruction for the letters are singnature.

The 'signature', which was kept a secret from the public, was a red circle and a blue circle, interlocking.

Sackloads of sympathy mail arrived for the Lindberghs – estimated at 200,000 letters and cards – and, after Mrs Lindbergh had broadcast instructions on how the baby was to be fed, a note arrived from the kidnapper telling her not to worry.

On 8 March Dr John F. Condon, a retired school principal from the Bronx,

published in the *Bronx Home News* a letter to the kidnapper offering to add $1,000 of his own to the ransom and act as a go-between for the parties 'so that a loving mother may again have her darling child'. Next morning he received a reply from the kidnapper and late at night on 12 March met him near Woodlawn Cemetery. The

Lindbergh's baby son during the celebrations for his first birthday.

The Lindbergh home after the kidnapping.

kidnapper, 'John', established his authenticity, and the two conducted a 'correspondence', in which Dr Condon's messages were carried in the newspaper's small ads column. The kidnapper sent the baby's suit to prove his authenticity further, and increased the ransom to $70,000.

On 2 April Dr Condon kept a rendezvous with 'John' at St Raymond's Cemetery. Colonel Lindbergh, who was waiting in a car with $70,000 in bills in a cardboard box, heard 'John's' voice calling to the doctor. 'John' did not have the baby, but he and the doctor agreed that he should accept $50,000, and next day by post Dr Condon would receive instructions on how to find the baby.

The money was paid, and the instructions read:

The boy is on the boad Nelly. It is a small boad 28 feet long. Two persons are on the board. They are innocent. You will find the boad between Horseneck Beach and Gay Head, near Elizabeth Island.

Lindbergh, Dr Condon and a friend flew to Massachusetts to find the boat, but it was a wild goose chase. There was no sign of a boat *Nelly*, nor had anyone heard of it. Knowing he had been tricked, Lindbergh informed the press of the events. The serial numbers of the notes of the ransom money, which, unknown to Lindbergh the Treasury had noted, were released.

On 12 May, about five miles from the Lindbergh home, the decomposing body of a baby was found in a shallow grave. The Lindbergh's nurse identified a rotting shirt as one she had made. Death had been from a blow on the head, and was estimated to have taken place two months earlier, i.e., soon after the kidnapping.

No progress was made in finding the criminal, although a member of the US Forestry Service performed wonders in tracing the wood used to make the ladder, from the forest it grew in to the timber yard in the Bronx which sold it. But that took 18 months and the trail led no further. A sad event arising from the intensive investigation was the suicide of a maid at the home of Mrs Lindbergh's family after persistent questioning, there being strong suspicions that the kidnapping must be an 'inside' job.

A suspect was finally found by luck. In May 1934 President Roosevelt abandoned the gold standard and proclaimed that all gold certificates issued by the government and in use as currency should be returned to the Treasury. Most of the ransom money had been in gold certificates.

On 18 September 1934 a gas station manager accepted a $10 gold certificate in payment and, as a precaution, since he knew such certificates should have been handed in, he took a note of the car registration number of the man who gave it to him. When he himself changed the certificate at the bank the teller checked and found it was from the ransom money. The car number was traced and it led to the suspect, a 36-year-old former German soldier, Bruno Hauptmann, who had entered the United States in 1923. He had had previous convictions in Germany and, when he was arrested on 19 September, another certificate from the ransom money was in his pocket. It was now 2½ years after the kidnapping.

Police took apart Hauptmann's house and garage and found some $14,000 of the ransom money, plus a revolver which, with some of the money, was hidden in a hollowed-out joist.

Hauptmann was brought to trial at Flemington, New Jersey, on 2 January 1935. Despite his and his devoted wife's protestations of innocence, he had no chance after the discovery of the money and the evidence of the handwriting ex-

Bruno Hauptmann in court flanked by a state trooper and a deputy sheriff.

perts. Hauptmann's defence was that the money belonged to a business partner, Isidor Fisch, who had returned to Germany, dying there in 1934. Hauptmann said he had recently discovered the money in a shoe box which Fisch had left in his care and, since Fisch had owed him $7,500, he had begun to use it.

The evidence in court was so strong, however, that Hauptmann was convicted and went to the electric chair on 3 April 1936.

There have since been theories that a miscarriage of justice may have taken place. At the time the prison governor, Harold Hoffmann, was impressed by Hauptmann's behaviour in the condemned cell, but everybody else was glad to get the awful crime 'solved'. It has been suggested that some vital evidence against Hauptmann may have been planted. There were certainly puzzling aspects of the case, not least the crude ladder which broke near the top, presumably endangering the kidnapper and the whole enterprise. Hauptmann was a professional carpenter and a good one.

An intriguing theory advanced by Theon Wright, an American reporter, was that the baby was not murdered at all. He suggested that the kidnapping was planned by Al Capone's friends in an effort to get him released from jail (Capone had, four months earlier, been sentenced to 11 years in prison for tax evasion.) This theory is supported by the fact that, at the time of the kidnapping, Capone had offered from his cell to get the baby restored to his parents if he were released. There is even a candidate for the Lindbergh baby. A businessman, Harold Olsen, was given to his 'parents' when a baby 'by gangsters', and grew up believing his real father might have been Al Capone. When an adult, he was told by his former nurse that he was, in fact, the Lindbergh baby. He is the right age and photographs show a strong similarity.

The 1940s

Burnt bodies,
mutilated bodies,
a missing body and
bodies dissolved in acid.

Crowds waiting outside Pentonville prison as Neville Heath is executed.

THE CURIOUS LITTLE ROOM

Was the French doctor working for the wartime resistance, or getting rich by murdering helpless fugitives?

On 11 March 1944 foul-smelling smoke was belching from a chimney at 32 rue Lesueur, Paris. The street was in a fashionable district, and the neighbours were not amused, particularly as nasty smuts were beginning to settle. One neighbour went to complain and, receiving no reply from the large house, rang the police. They discovered that the house belonged to Dr

Petiot's secret cellar where the bodies of his victims were treated with quicklime.

Marcel Petiot, whose practice was nearby, in rue Caumartin, so they sent for him and for the fire brigade, who immediately broke into the premises.

The source of the smoke was a furnace in the basement, and the shocked firemen discovered that it was fuelled by human bodies. But they had already been appalled and sickened before peering into the furnace, for all around it were dismembered corpses. Heads, torsos, arms and legs were scattered about waiting to be added to the flames.

Dr Petiot arrived, and told the police that all the corpses were those of Germans or of Nazi collaborators. All were known to the French resistance, he asserted, and their executions were carried out for the honour of France. Paris, at the time, was still under German occupation, with the resistance bravely trying to save patriotic Frenchmen from the Gestapo, the German secret police. Petiot's story was convincing enough to save him from instant arrest, and he immediately fled Paris and took refuge in the countryside where, in the chaos of wartime, it was not difficult to avoid detection.

The bones in the grisly house were pieced together by forensic experts, who decided that they belonged to 27 people.

Much was discovered about Petiot and his activities in the following months, and rumours began to circulate that he himself was a Nazi collaborator. Petiot was moved to write a letter to the newspaper *Résistance* in order to rebut these accusations and to claim that the Nazis had framed him by dumping the bodies round the furnace while the Gestapo had him under arrest.

The Petiot case was an urgent priority for the police in the days after the liberation and, when a disguised Petiot returned to Paris for the celebrations, he was arrested and charged with 27 murders.

Petiot's defence was simple. He denied eight of the killings, admitted 19 and added another 44, making 63 victims by his own admission. But all, he declared, were traitors and collaborators, executed by himself as a hero of the resistance.

Petiot was a dark and good-looking 49-year-old in 1946 when his trial began. He was confident of winning his case and was witty and cocky in court. He stood for France, he proclaimed, and in those post-war days of recriminations and the settling of scores, there were many to believe him and to support him.

However, the summary of his life, which was read out by the president of the court, was enough to make anybody suspicious.

He had been born in Auxerre in 1897 and, while serving in an army casualty clearing station in Dijon during the First World War, had been court-martialled for stealing drugs for morphia addicts. He was acquitted and sent to an asylum for psychiatric treatment. There he studied medicine and in 1921 qualified as a doctor. He began practising at Villeneuve-sur-Yonne, where in 1927 he became mayor.

He built up a profitable business, partly by supplying illegal drugs and by performing abortions. He was thought to be having an affair with his pretty young housekeeper, who became pregnant and disappeared. In 1930 he was accused of murdering a local shopkeeper, a patient, who was robbed, but nothing could be proved, even when another patient, who was active in the accusations, died suddenly and unexpectedly. Petiot provided the death certificate and recorded the death as natural.

In 1936 he moved to Paris and began a lucrative practice at rue Caumartin. He was again in trouble for supplying drugs and was caught stealing, but avoided imprisonment by undertaking psychiatric treatment. There was also another mysterious disappearance of an accuser – this time a woman who claimed that he had ruined her daughter with his drug-peddling activities. However, it was when the Nazis occupied Paris in 1940 that Petiot, according to the prosecution at his trial, began his biggest profit-making venture.

He bought the mansion at rue Lesueur and fitted it up for his purposes, installing

the furnace and a soundproof triangular room with one door and no windows (but there were peepholes).

Petiot let it be known that he belonged to the resistance and was able to help Jews and patriots wanted by the Gestapo to escape to Spain. Desperate men, sometimes accompanied by wives and families, came for help. He persuaded them to sell their belongings to pay for their freedom, and then received them into his mansion, gave them their 'inoculations' and sat them in his triangular room. The injections were lethal, and when they were dead he placed the bodies in quicklime in the cellar, until they were ready for the furnace.

The beauty of Petiot's scheme was that his ill-gotten gains were brought to him by people who, because they were escaping the Gestapo, were meticulous in covering up their tracks. Ironically, however, the Gestapo discovered a link between Petiot and Jews who disappeared while being sought by them. They suspected Petiot of being the resistance agent he was pretending to be and set him a trap. A Gestapo man posed as an escapee and went to Petiot. Like the others, he disappeared.

Petiot was arrested by the Gestapo and held for months before being released in 1944. There has been subsequent speculation as to why he was released. It has been suggested that he convinced the Nazis that, by eliminating their enemies,

Below
Examining exhibits used in the prosecution's case against Petiot.

the gruesome business, had refused to have anything more to do with it. Petiot was subsequently forced to burn his bodies without the flesh being previously rotted by quicklime, and this produced the evil-smelling black smoke to which his neighbours objected.

Many of Petiot's victims were identified, partly because he kept a notebook of payments, partly because their families knew they had reported to Petiot and partly because of no fewer than 1,700 articles of clothing found in 47 suitcases in a house in Villeneuve – suitcases which, witnesses confirmed, had been taken from rue Lesueur by Petiot's brother.

Petiot maintained throughout his trial that all his genuine clients had escaped and

Left
Accompanied by detectives, Petiot returns to his Paris home to take part in a 'reconstruction of the crime'.
Below
Petiot in court (centre left). The details of the case were avidly followed by a crowd of spectators.

he was actually a very efficient partner in their business.

It was this arrest by the Gestapo, however, that brought about Petiot's eventual downfall. Previously he had been obtaining his quicklime from his brother, Maurice, but Maurice had visited rue Lesueur while Petiot was under detention and, discovering the scale and nature of

that the bodies belonged to traitors. But no escapees came forward, no letters were sent from Spain or South America and no resistance workers appeared to confirm Petiot as a colleague. He was found guilty, a verdict he had to ask to be repeated because the commotion in court prevented it being heard. On 26 May 1946 he faced the guillotine, still cocky and joking.

AN OFFICER AND A GENTLEMAN

He seemed to be a gallant officer, handsome and attentive, but he was a vicious sadist.

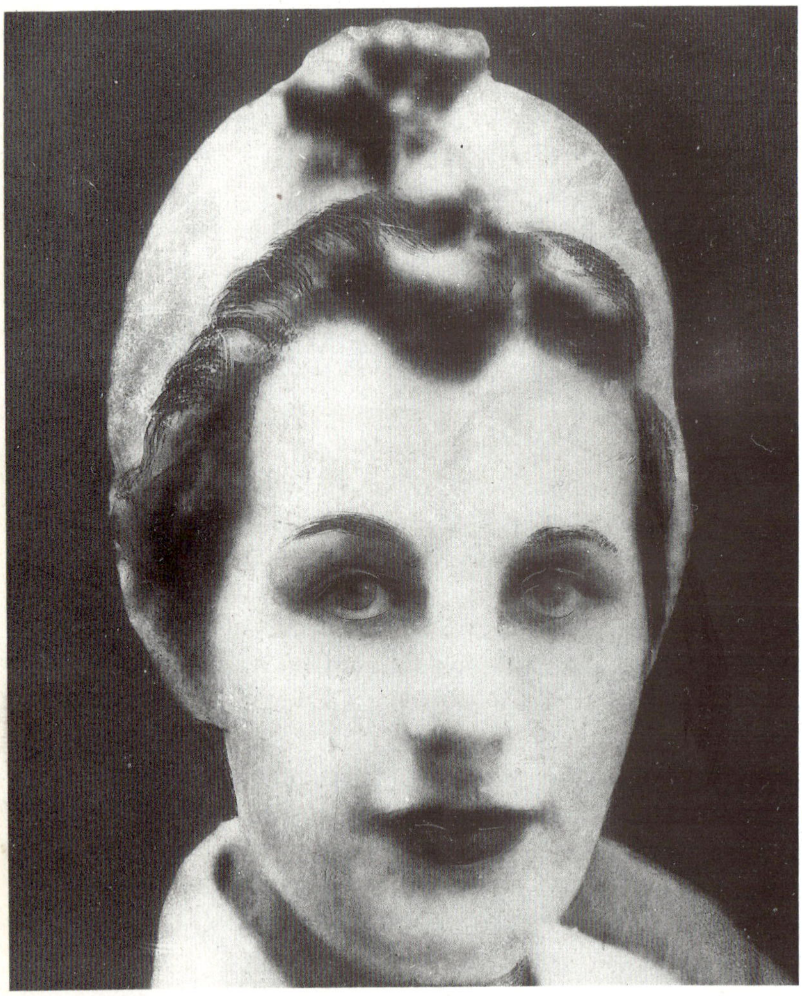

Margery Gardner, murdered by Heath in a London hotel.

When handsome, six-foot, 29-year-old ex-officer and wartime pilot Neville George Clevely Heath met Miss Yvonne Symonds at a dance in Chelsea in midsummer 1946 he took her to the Panama Club in South Kensington, but later she declined to spend the night with him. The next day, however, after he had proposed marriage and she had accepted, they did spend the night together, in Room 4 of the Pembridge Court Hotel in Notting Hill, signing the register as 'Mr and Mrs N.G.C. Heath'.

Soon afterwards Miss Symonds joined her parents in the seaside resort of Worthing, and a few days later Heath followed her, booking in at the Ocean Hotel. While dining and dancing at the Blue Peter Club in nearby Angmering, Heath told Miss Symonds of a dreadful murder that had occurred the previous week in the same room in which they had stayed. Heath, according to his account, had known the victim, a young film extra, Mrs Margery Gardner, and had lent her his key on meeting her with a man looking for a place to sleep. Naturally he had explained that to a Chief Inspector Barratt, who was investigating the crime, and who had later taken

Heath in the company of police officers.

him to the room and shown him the body. Miss Symonds wanted to know how the girl had been killed and Heath was quite blunt. 'A poker was stuck up her,' he said. 'I suppose the man was a sex maniac'.

So far as it went, Heath's account was accurate, apart from the claim that Chief Inspector (really Superintendent) Barratt had interviewed him and shown him the body. What Heath did not tell Miss Symonds was that the police were looking for him. She discovered this next day from the Sunday newspapers. She immediately rang him and he promised her he would drive straight back to London to sort things out and call her back that evening. He never did.

A week earlier, the true sequence of events after the murder at the Pembridge Court Hotel was that a darkened Room 4 was entered at 2 pm. One bed was covered in blood, with markings on the pillow suggesting that a blood-stained whip had lain there. On the other bed, covered up, was the mutilated body of Margery Gardner, who had been savagely attacked with whip and teeth by a person rightly described by Heath as a maniac. The ultimate cause of death was suffocation.

The police had no difficulty in deciding they wanted Heath to 'help with inquiries' (the room was in his name), nor did they have difficulty in piecing together his life, for he had a criminal record. Commissioned in the Royal Air Force in 1936 at the age of 19, he had been court-martialled and dismissed for various offences, and then sent to Borstal for housebreaking, stealing and forgery. On the outbreak of war he was released and commissioned in the Royal Army Services Corps. Court-martialled again a year later for numerous offences in the Far East, he escaped at Durban, South Africa, from the ship bringing him home. He enlisted in the South African Air Force under the name Armstrong, was commissioned for a third time and, ironically, seconded to the RAF in England as a bomber pilot. Back in South Africa he was court-martialled yet again and dismissed the service, and he arrived back in Britain in February 1946. In April he was fined at Wimbledon, where he lived, for wearing a military uniform with decorations, passing himself off as a serving officer.

It was not difficult, either, for the police to discover that the night before the murder Heath and Margery Gardner had danced at the Panama Club and gone on by taxi to the Pembridge Court Hotel.

While police stations and the public all over Britain were asked to look for Heath, the police investigating the murder, who had found photographs of him in his home, did not request that his picture be published in the newspapers, since it could prejudice his trial, identification being a crucial factor. It was a mistake which possibly cost another life as the smoothly attractive killer struck again.

Heath did not return to London that Sunday after leaving his fiancée. He went to the Tollard Royal Hotel in the genteel resort of Bournemouth, passing as Group Captain Rupert Brooke, a name guaranteed to attract attention, as Rupert Brooke was a famous handsome soldier-poet who had died young during the First World War. Heath wrote to 'Chief Inspector' Barratt at New Scotland Yard to repeat his story of having lent his keys to Margery Gardner and a man (he provided a description). In this version of the story, however, he had returned to his room at around 3 am, found the body and fled in panic. He said he would forward the 'instrument' with which the victim was beaten, but did not.

On 3 July the charming and gentlemanly 'Group Captain' met a pretty 21-year-old ex-Wren, Doreen Marshall, on the promenade, and gave her tea, and later dinner, at his hotel. In the lounge, after midnight, other guests noticed that Heath was slightly drunk, and Miss Marshall ordered a taxi back to her own hotel, the nearby Norfolk. However, on Heath's insistence, she allowed him to walk her home, Heath telling the night porter he would be half-an-hour. When he had not returned by 4.30 am the porter glanced into his room. Heath was asleep, having used the fire escape and a ladder to get into his room unobserved. He was subsequently to claim that it was a joke on the porter.

A day or so later the manager of the Norfolk Hotel rang his counterpart at the Tollard Royal to say that his guest, Miss Marshall, was missing, and that he understood she had dined at the Tollard Royal just before her disappearance. Such was

Right
Police searching in Branksome Chine where Doreen Marshall's body was found.

Heath's convincing presence, however, that this fact was not put to him for several hours, and his insistence that the girl he had entertained was not Doreen Marshall was immediately accepted.

Heath then rang the local police station to ask if he could come round to look at a picture of Miss Marshall, to be sure that she had not been his guest. Throughout the search for him Heath had acted with a confidence that bordered on recklessness. At the Pembridge Court Hotel and at Worthing he had used his own name. Perhaps he knew he would be ultimately caught but it amused him to push his luck outrageously. Now he paid what he expected to be a quick visit (he was without a jacket) to the local police station. He was immediately recognized as Heath (although he insisted he was Brooke) and detained. When the police sent for his jacket, at his request, they found in it a ticket which led them to a suitcase he had deposited at Bournemouth railway station. In it was a bloodstained scarf and a leather riding whip with a metal tip, of the kind that had been used to beat Mrs Gardner. They also found the return half of Doreen Marshall's railway ticket from London and an artificial pearl, later shown to have come from her necklace. It was soon discovered that Heath had pawned Doreen Marshall's ring, and in his room was found a bloodstained, knotted handkerchief with human hairs attached to it.

Left
Doreen Marshall. Heath entertained her to dinner at his hotel before brutally murdering her.

Heath had taken to wearing a silk scarf, and when it was found that this hid scratches on his neck, he seemed doomed. However, he insisted he had seen Doreen Marshall home and that she had told him she was leaving town.

Two days after Heath had walked into the police station, Doreen Marshall's body was found by a walker who noticed the cloud of flies above it. It was in Branksome Chine. She was naked, with her hands tied, and had been savagely mutilated. Her throat had been cut and her clothing had been used to cover the body.

At Heath's trial, at which he did not give evidence, the only possible plea was insanity, but the jury took less than an hour to decide that he was guilty.

Heath, smartly dressed, debonair and arrogant, maintained his officer-and-gentleman control to the last. He wrote to his mother to say that he would sit up during his last night in order to see the dawn, which he associated happily with early morning aircraft patrols and coming home late from night clubs. On 26 October 1946, not long after seeing his last dawn, he was hanged.

A MURDER WITHOUT A BODY

What happened to the beautiful actress after her last cigarette one hot night on the promenade deck?

The SS *Durban Castle* in which Gay Gibson made her last trip.

A murder charge without a body is always a difficult one to prove, and when the alleged murder takes place at sea there is the added problem that the evidence may disappear along with the body. In 1948, however, there was just enough evidence to make life uncomfortable for James Camb, accused of murder on an ocean liner.

The alleged victim was a beautiful actress, Eileen Isabella Ronnie Gibson, known professionally as Gay Gibson. She had been born in 1926 in India, where her father was a successful businessman, but had been sent back to England for her education. During the Second World War she had joined the ATS, the women's army corps. Interested in the stage, she had managed to join a services theatrical company, 'Stars in Battledress', which toured round giving performances for the troops. After the war she and her mother joined her father in South Africa, where he was then working, and she attempted to further her stage career in Johannesburg. She did well, and very soon was playing the lead in a play called *The Man with a Load of Mischief*. The title role was played by Eric Boon, near the end of a boxing career in which he had been an outstanding British lightweight champion, and at the beginning of a less successful acting career.

Unfortunately for Gay Gibson the play's run came to an end, and she decided to go back to England in order to try her luck in the West End. On 10 October 1947 she set sail in the SS *Durban Castle*, leaving Cape Town for Southampton.

What happened during the first week of the voyage, after which she disappeared,

Above left
Gay Gibson. Her ill-fated voyage home was prompted by a desire to pursue her acting career.
Below left
James Camb. The prosecution alleged that he strangled Gay Gibson when she resisted him.

was to come out in court, when on 18 March 1948 the trial for murder of handsome, 31-year-old James Camb began at the Assize Court at Winchester.

It seems that Gay Gibson immediately attracted the attention of Camb, the promenade deck steward who, although a married man with a child, was known to have a liking for cruise romances. Camb told the stewardess assigned to Gay Gibson's cabin that the actress had confided in him that she was three-months pregnant. The stewardess thought Camb was merely trying to enlist her aid in getting to know Miss Gibson and, on seeing him later near her cabin, warned him that she would report anything untoward, since Camb's duties were on the promenade deck, and he was not permitted to enter the passengers' cabins.

Gay Gibson in fact led a rather sedate life on board. Her usual companions at dinner were a Mr Hopwood, an official of the shipping line, and a Wing Commander Bray. These were the people with whom she dined on 17 October, after which she danced a little and then retired to her cabin, in order, she said, to change into a swimming costume for a dip in the pool, since it was a very hot night. However, she soon returned, saying she could not find her costume, and finally retired at 12.40 am, Mr Hopwood escorting her to her cabin as usual.

However, it appears that Gay Gibson did not look for a swimsuit when she left the dancehall, for the nightwatchman saw her talking to Camb on the promenade deck. Neither did she retire at 12.40, despite being taken to her cabin, because the boatswain's mate saw her and spoke to her at one o'clock, when she was still in her evening dress, smoking on the afterdeck.

That was the last time Gay Gibson was seen, alive or dead, except, it was alleged, by Camb.

At 3 am a cabin bell rang. At that time of night it was the job of the nightwatchman or his assistant to investigate, and the assistant, Frederick Steer, went to B deck where he saw it was Miss Gibson, in Cabin 126, who had rung. In fact, when he reached the cabin, he realized, from the fact that the lights were on outside her door, that she had rung the bells for both a steward and a stewardess.

As Steer went to enter the door was slammed in his face, but not before he had seen and heard Camb, who told him everything was all right. Steer thought he had better report the incident to the nightwatchman, James Murray, and together they returned to the cabin, but all was now quiet. However Murray, without naming Camb, related what had happened to the officer of the watch, who decided it was a private matter and not the concern of the ship's officers.

At 7.30 am the stewardess discovered

The porthole, a vital piece of evidence, being carried into court.

the door of cabin 126 unlocked, which was most unusual, and when she could not find its occupant, she reported her absence to Captain Patey. He ordered the ship to be searched, and when there was no sign of Gay Gibson he turned the ship round in order to search the sea, reporting the loss of a passenger to other nearby vessels. But the captain soon had to give up the hopeless task.

Steer now informed the captain of Camb's presence in the cabin. Camb was questioned and denied being there, but agreed to be examined by the ship's surgeon, Dr Griffiths, who found scratches on his shoulders and arms.

When the *Durban Castle* reached Southampton, Camb was interviewed by police and eventually admitted that he had been in the cabin. His new story was that Gay Gibson had died during sexual intercourse, to which she had consented. She had had a little fit, had clutched at him, had foamed at the mouth a little and was then still. He had panicked and pushed her body through the porthole.

The prosecution's allegation at the trial was that Camb had strangled Gay Gibson either when she resisted his advances, or else to avoid her charging him with rape or attempted rape. Their main evidence was the scratches on his body (photographed at Southampton), Gay Gibson's blood found on sheets and a pillowslip, a contraceptive appliance which Gay Gibson had not used (the implication was that she would have used it if intercourse had been with her consent, as Camb claimed) and an extended confession which Camb was alleged to have made to the police officer who took his fingerprints:

'She struggled. I had my hands around her neck.... I threw her out of the porthole.'

Camb denied making this statement and brought witnesses to suggest that Gay Gibson was the sort of girl likely to agree to intercourse with him, and that she suffered from an illness which might have led her to have difficulty in breathing at times of excitement. From South Africa came the actor-producer who had engaged Gay Gibson, who said she suffered from asthma, and a fellow actor who swore she had fainting fits similar to the one from which Camb claimed she had died. The actor-producer's wife, a doctor, said that Miss Gibson had hinted that she might be pregnant. The other defence witnesses were pathologists who said that Camb's description of the actress's death was feasible. There was also a story that a man had given Gay Gibson £500, but her mother swore it was a business proposition to back her in her career. It is difficult to know what other supporting evidence Camb could bring, but his confession, and the fact that he had changed his story weighed heavily with the judge, and the jury took only three-quarters of an hour to find him guilty.

Camb was sentenced to death, but escaped hanging. The House of Commons tried to add a clause to the Criminal Justice Bill, which was then being debated, suspending the death penalty for five years. The House of Lords rejected the clause, but the home secretary decided to commute to life imprisonment all death sentences which were pending in the interim.

Three other women subsequently came forward to claim Camb had tried to force his attentions on them during voyages, one actually describing an attempted strangulation. Nevertheless, Camb was released on licence in 1959. He changed his name and became a head waiter, but after a few years was in trouble again for sexual misbehaviour with young girls and was sent back to prison to continue his sentence.

THE ACID-BATH MURDERER

He drank his victim's blood and dissolved her body in acid, but her dentures told a grisly tale.

Mrs Olive Henrietta Helen Olivia Robarts Durand-Deacon not only possessed a wealth of names, she also had some £40,000 – a legacy from her late husband, a colonel in the Gloucestershire Regiment. Although 69 and well-off, she was not one to sit back in genteel retirement. She designed some artificial fingernails and hoped to market them.

This ambition seemed a little nearer fulfilment when a young man at her hotel, the Onslow Court, in the respectable museum area of London's South Kensington, offered to help. A self-employed engineer, he suggested they could look at some plastics at his factory in Crawley, Sussex, and they arranged a trip there for 18 February 1949.

The man was the courtly and handsome John George Haigh. He was well-dressed and personable, and his attentive manners had already charmed the elderly widows who formed much of the clientele at the Onslow Court.

Unfortunately for Mrs Durand-Deacon the 39-year-old man with the trim moustache was not what he seemed and the trip to Crawley was to be her last. Perhaps she should have been warned when, instead of picking her up from the hotel, Haigh met her outside the Army and Navy Stores in Victoria Street, some distance away.

Mrs Durand-Deacon settled down in Haigh's smart Alvis car and no doubt enjoyed the 30-mile journey to Crawley, as well as tea in the George Hotel. However, the factory was probably a disappointment. It was small and, in fact, was not Haigh's – he merely had the use of a storeroom to carry out his experiments. It was late on Friday afternoon, and Haigh and Mrs Durand-Deacon had the place to themselves.

Above
John George Haigh, who exercised a baleful charm over elderly ladies.
Left
Mrs Durand-Deacon whose remains Haigh reduced to a greasy sludge.

What the wealthy widow did not know was that Haigh had made deadly preparations for this visit. A 45-gallon drum was to hand, lined to hold strong chemicals, and Haigh had bought a carboy of sulphuric acid. A rubber apron, gloves and pump were also set out on a bench, like a surgeon's instruments in an operating theatre. The unsuspecting Mrs Durand-Deacon had little time to take all this in, for on entering the room Haigh produced a revolver from his pocket and killed her with an expert shot through the back of the neck.

According to Haigh's story his next action also had the precision of a surgical operation. He made a careful incision in an artery in her neck with a sharp knife and, as the warm blood pumped out, he filled a glass and drank.

Having stripped the body, Haigh then laid down the drum, pushed his victim's head and shoulders in and then, with his feet standing on the bottom end of the drum, i.e. at the other end, he could lever it upright by pulling at the rim. The body, much heavier than his own 140-lb frame, came up with the drum and sank inside.

Wearing his rubber clothing, Haigh poured in the acid and left it to do its work over the weekend. Tea, poached egg and toast, and a joke or two with the proprietor of the nearby Ye Olde Ancient Priors Restaurant preceded a drive back to the Onslow Court Hotel.

It was now that Haigh discovered that the little bit of bad luck which often catches criminals had befallen him. Mrs Durand-Deacon's disappearance had not, of course, been unnoticed, and at breakfast on Saturday he learned that, while preparing to leave for her fatal excursion, she had met her friend, Mrs Constance Lane, in the hotel foyer, and had confided in her the purpose of the trip.

On Saturday morning Haigh hurriedly sold the jewellery he had taken from Mrs Durand-Deacon's body and took her fur coat to a cleaner's.

On Sunday Mrs Lane insisted that they should jointly report Mrs Durand-Deacon's disappearance to the authorities. They went to the police station where he gave an account of the arrangement he had made with Mrs Durand-Deacon, stating that he had waited an hour for her at the appointed time, that she had not turned up and that he had gone to Crawley alone.

Haigh was thanked and later that day returned to Crawley, where he poured the remains of Mrs Durand-Deacon – now sludge – into a hole in the ground near the storeroom and covered them.

However, he was now near capture. A woman police-sergeant who interviewed the guests at the Onslow Court had an uneasy feeling about him. Her superior wondered if he had a record – and sure enough discovered that Haigh had served sentences for fraud and theft. The following Saturday the police took a look at the Crawley storeroom and found the pump, acid, a blood-stained apron and a recently fired revolver. Haigh was soon once again at the police station – this time by invitation.

Realizing that the game was up, he began to prepare the ground for a defence of insanity. He challenged the police to find any trace of Mrs Durand-Deacon in the sludge to which he directed them. Unfortunately for him they did. Her dentures were intact and readily identified. Haigh now

Donald McSwan (right) and Dr and Mrs Archibald Henderson (far right) were among Haigh's victims.

Haigh leaves court after the first day's hearing of his case.

confessed to previous murders in the preceding five years: Donald McSwan in 1944, McSwan's parents soon afterwards and, in 1948, a Dr Archibald Henderson and his wife. From each victim, Haigh claimed, he had taken his glass of blood before dissolving the bodies in acid. Investigation showed that these people, indeed, had been murdered.

The London *Daily Mirror* got hold of these sensational stories and informed their readers about the 'Vampire'. This brought an action for contempt of court which earned the newspaper a fine and the editor a spell of imprisonment, but aroused tremendous public interest.

Haigh was tried at Lewes, Sussex, in July 1949 and sentenced to death after a 15-minute retirement by the jury. His plea was insanity, of course, and from his death cell he tried to explain how his mind had been shaped. His parents were Plymouth Brethren, and at the age of 12 he was a choirboy in Wakefield Cathedral. However, he claimed that his parents, though loving, inhibited his behaviour, just as they inhibited his freedom with a high wall round their house. His father carried a scar on his forehead as the result of an accident and said it was the 'mark of Satan' for a sinner. Haigh told of boyhood dreams of crucifixes and blood, and how, after a car accident in 1944 in which his own blood had flowed down his face and into his mouth, the dreams had returned.

On the other hand, Haigh, in debt to bookmakers, had shown remarkable skill in forging letters in his victims' names, fooling personal and business acquaintances sufficiently to allay suspicion and to acquire their property. The real state of his mind will never be known.

GARAGE
CHARRING

The 1950s

A houseful of corpses,
two cold-blooded killers,
a jealous mistress,
and dishonour among thieves.

A crowd stands silently outside Holloway prison as Ruth Ellis is executed.

THE BODIES AT 10 RILLINGTON PLACE

A wife and baby were murdered, and a husband hanged – but it was all a mistake.

On 24 March 1953 the bodies of a number of women were found in a house, 10 Rillington Place, in London's Notting Hill area. A John Christie had recently been living there and a warrant was issued for his arrest on suspicion of murder.

It so happened that, four years earlier, two other bodies had been found in the house, those of a woman and a baby. They belonged to a family of three to whom Christie had sub-let the room on the floor above his. The husband, an illiterate van-driver, Timothy Evans, had been charged with the murders, and convicted and hanged for the murder of the baby. He had confessed, but had later withdrawn the confession and had accused Christie of the crimes. Christie and his wife had been witnesses for the prosecution. With the discovery of the new bodies, many began to believe that Evans' conviction could have been a miscarriage of justice. Was it likely, they said, that two murderers, acting independently, were living in the same house? Surely it was more likely that the earlier bodies had belonged to victims of the same mass-murderer?

Christie was discovered a few days later standing on Putney Bridge, staring at the Thames. He had been living rough and seemed almost relieved to be caught. He soon confessed to six murders – but denied involvement in the deaths of Mrs Evans and the baby. Later, in prison awaiting his execution, he confessed to killing Mrs Evans but still protested his innocence as regards the baby.

John Reginald Halliday Christie, born in 1898 in Yorkshire, grew into a short-

Police carry a coffin away from 10 Rillington Place.

Right
Christie in his wartime uniform as a special constable.
Below right
Ruth Fuerst, Christie's first victim, was buried in his garden.

sighted, inadequate youth whose stern father threw him out of the house when he was convicted of pilfering. In his teens he suffered humiliation when he was unable to have sexual intercourse with a girl. She related the incident to their acquaintances and he became known as 'Reggie No-Dick'. Towards the end of the First World War he enlisted in the army and suffered a dose of mustard gas poisoning. From then on he spoke in a soft voice, which he would sometimes lose altogether in periods of nervous hysteria. He married in 1920 but continued to have sexual inhibitions. In 1934 he suffered head injuries when knocked down by a car.

Yet Christie was not retiring. He became a member of the Halifax Conservative Association and boasted about former wealth. He could be violent when his frustrations built up, and he had a conviction for a vicious assault on a girl. Christie was a man who needed to be looked up to and the most successful period of his life began in 1939 when he became a war reserve policeman. By then he and his wife Ethel had moved to London and had taken the ground floor flat in 10 Rillington Place – now one of the most famous addresses in British criminal history.

Christie enjoyed his power as a policeman, although he was far from being a friendly neighbourhood 'bobby' – he was a stickler for the rule book. One day in 1943 when his wife was away Constable Christie met Ruth Fuerst in a cafe. She was suffering from a cold, and he told her he had an ideal cure for a blocked nose, inviting her to 10 Rillington Place to try it. It involved breathing through a tube the steam from a bowl of boiling water to which had been added various proprietary cold cures. The bowl was covered with a cloth, 'to keep the steam in', but what Ruth Fuerst did not know was that the tube was also connected to the gas tap. When she became unconscious Christie raped her and then strangled her. It was to become a pattern with Christie and his victims. Incapable of intercourse with a conscious woman, he would satisfy his pent-up desires in a frenzy of activity with the unconscious or dead body – sometimes for

days – before disposing of the corpse.

Ruth Fuerst was buried in the garden. In 1944 Mrs Christie was again away – visiting relatives in Yorkshire – and Christie had another orgy of satisfaction with her friend, Muriel Eady. She, too, was buried in the garden before his wife's return.

In 1949 came the murder of Beryl Evans. The Evans family had come to live on an upstairs floor and Evans, who was poor, told Christie that his wife was pregnant again (they had a baby daughter, Geraldine) and that they wanted an abortion, at that time illegal. Christie told Evans that he had trained as a doctor and that, as a

favour, he would perform the operation. Christie had first aid manuals on his shelves and the illiterate Evans was convinced of his credentials. One morning while Evans was at work, Christie began the 'operation' on the compliant Beryl. He persuaded her to relax by inhaling some gas, and then raped and strangled her.

He now had to admit to his wife that the abortion had gone wrong and, on Evans' return from work, he had to tell him the same story. He convinced the mentally sub-normal Evans that he (Evans) would be suspected of murder if the police knew of his wife's death and persuaded him to flee. Christie promised to hide the body in a large drain outside the house and to make sure the baby was safe by placing her with a couple he knew who would unofficially adopt her for the time being. Evans agreed to this and fled to Wales, where he stayed with relatives.

Evans found it difficult to answer enquiries about the whereabouts of his wife. The strain of being on the run became so much for him that, on 30 November 1949, he went to Merthyr Tydfil police station and told them where to find the body of his wife – in the drain outside 10 Rillington Place. Police investigated, but there was no body. Evans under questioning confessed to murdering her and claimed that Christie had helped him dispose of the body down the drain, but it was only on a third visit to the house that the police found the body. Ironically, they had been standing in the garden discussing with the very helpful Christie the possibility of digging it up. Only Christie knew that two other bodies were also buried there – with the possible exception of Christie's little dog, which was digging around at the time. Christie was forced to send the animal indoors. Legend has it that the dog had uncovered a bone and that Christie was obliged to kick the earth back over it.

The garden was not dug because a detective meanwhile investigated an outside washroom and found the body of Beryl Evans behind some boards under a sink. Behind her body was that of the baby,

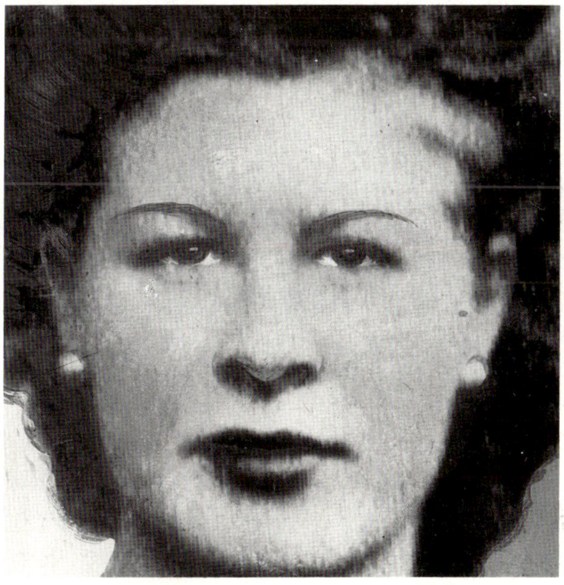

Above left
Christie with his wife, Ethel.
Far left
Muriel Eady, whom Christie murdered while his wife was away on a visit.
Left
Rita Nelson, a prostitute, who joined the growing list of Christie's victims.

Above
Police digging in the garden at 10 Rillington Place.
Right
Timothy Evans on his way to prison under police escort.

strangled with one of Evans' ties. Evans was shattered to discover his baby dead, and now accused Christie of both murders.

Evans was tried for the murder of his daughter in 1950. His defence was that Christie was responsible for the death of his wife as described and had probably murdered the baby, too, after persuading Evans to flee.

Christie's previous convictions did not come out at the trial, where the judge complimented him on the way he presented his evidence. He was seen as the unfortunate innocent on whom Evans was desperately trying to foist the crime. Evans was found guilty and hanged on 9 March 1950.

Christie's relationship with his wife Ethel was now very precarious. She either knew he was a murderer or at least had strong suspicions about him. Moreover, his appetite for unusual sexual adventures had probably increased with the affair of Mrs Evans and the fact that he had got away with murder. The presence of his wife was, therefore, a hindrance to further orgies. In December 1952 Christie decided to dispose of Ethel. He strangled her and hid her body below the floorboards in the dining room.

Christie then embarked on what might be seen as the last fling of a doomed man. During the next three months three more bodies were added to the gruesome collection at 10 Rillington Place. Christie was by now out of work, having lost his job as a post office clerk. He had no money and was steadily selling his furniture. He was, moreover, having to invent stories to account for the absence of his wife to satisfy both the neighbours and her relatives in Yorkshire.

Rita Nelson, a prostitute, was taken to the house in January 1953 where she shared the fate of Christie's previous victims. This body was merely wrapped in a

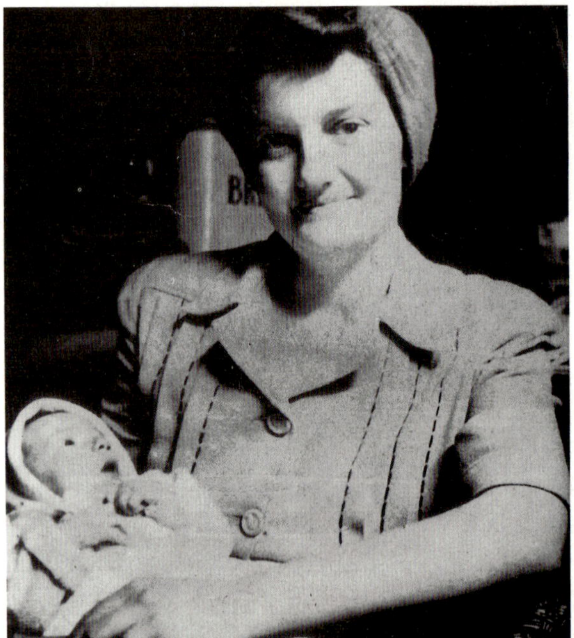

Right
Beryl Evans with her daughter Geraldine, for whose murder Evans was hanged.

blanket and placed in a cupboard for when Christie decided he needed another. Kathleen Maloney, also a prostitute, was next and she, too, ended in the cupboard, wrapped in a blanket.

Christie subsequently allowed an Irish couple to sleep in the flat for one night. On the next day the woman, Hectorina McLennan, was persuaded to return and she proved to be the final victim in the house of horror. Christie must now have felt that his whole situation was desperate. To flee was probably a decision which made his arrest certain, but to stay would no doubt have only delayed it. The last corpse was placed in the cupboard – in effect it was a recess. This body he did not wrap up, but merely tied a strip of blanket to the brassiere, which was still on the body, and fixed the other end to the wall, so that the body would not fall over. The other two bodies were in standing positions behind it. Christie then wall-papered over the cupboard door to disguise its existence and left the flat without notice.

A few days later a prospective new tenant, Mr Beresford Brown, was wondering where to fix a shelf for a radio set when he was surprised by the apparently hollow wall. Stripping aside some of the paper, he shone a torch through a hole in the cupboard door beneath and saw the apparently naked body of a woman. The police were called, and a thorough search of the premises revealed the five other bodies. A bizarre detail was that a thigh bone was propping a fence in the back garden where detectives had stood less than four years earlier.

Christie was tried for the murder of his wife, found guilty and hanged on 15 July 1953. He never did admit to killing Evans' daughter.

Nevertheless there was considerable concern that Timothy Evans had been wrongly hanged. Scott Henderson, QC, was appointed by the home secretary to enquire into the deaths of Mrs Evans and her baby. He found that the evidence against Evans was overwhelming. This satisfied only those who are always reluctant to admit that a miscarriage of justice has taken place.

In 1961 a book by the investigative journalist Ludovic Kennedy, *Ten Rillington Place*, presented a conclusive argument that there had in fact been a miscarriage of justice. In support of this he cited evidence obtained by the police that had not been passed to Evans' solicitor at the time, including the worksheets of men working in the house that had since mysteriously disappeared. The assumption was that, having convinced themselves of Evans' guilt, the police were lax in investigating anything which might lead to doubt.

In 1966 public pressure prompted another government review of the case under Mr Justice Brabin. It concluded that the balance of probabilities was that Evans killed his wife but not his child. As he had been convicted of murdering his child, it meant that he could be given a royal pardon, and his body could be taken from Pentonville prison and reburied in consecrated ground. It seemed about as far as the state was prepared to go in admitting a serious error on the part of the judiciary or the police. For the time being it had to satisfy Evans' family.

Juliet Hulme (right) and Pauline Rieper.

THEY WANTED TO GO TO SOUTH AFRICA

The two girls lived for each other, and the mother of one had to die for their obsession.

'The most glorious beings in creation,
They'd be the pride and joy of any nation,
Why are men such fools they will not realize
The wisdom that is hidden behind those strange eyes.
And these wonderful people are you and I.'

These were lines from a poem that two highly intelligent young girls of 15 and 16 from Christchurch, New Zealand, had written together. Called 'The Ones That I Worship', it was about themselves. They worshipped each other. Theirs was a lesbian relationship and they sought to be together always.

Pauline Rieper, the older girl, was the third of four children. The first, a 'blue baby', had died soon after birth and the fourth suffered from Down's syndrome. She herself had spent much of her early life in hospital. Her real name was actually Parker, since her mother, known as Mrs Honora Rieper, had not married her father, with whom she had been living for 25 years.

Her younger friend was Juliet Hulme, whose father had recently resigned as rector of Canterbury University College. She had been born in England in 1938, and had lived through part of the blitz on London during the Second World War, which had left her prone to nightmares. The family had moved to New Zealand after the war.

The girls were together whenever possible. They wrote novels as well as poems – novels full of sex and violence. In their plans to remain together for life, they had considered fleeing to America and, with no other career apparently open to them, to live by prostitution. Pauline had experimented with a boy to see how feasible sexual intercourse was. One night her father found the boy in her bed. Pauline's diary gave details of other fund-raising schemes the pair had tried, such as shoplifting and blackmailing the Hulme's new lodger.

Their families soon became aware of this unhealthy relationship, which was cutting each girl off from a normal home life, and

Mrs Rieper called on the Hulmes to discuss it. Dr Hulme, who had at first welcomed the friendship because Juliet was so shy, admitted his serious concern. He resolved to take Juliet to South Africa and split up the two girls. Naturally, when they got wind of the proposed move Juliet badgered her father to take Pauline, too, while Pauline came to fear that her mother might prevent it.

In April 1954 Pauline's diary, in which she was extremely frank, revealed that she had thought of a means of ridding herself of this obstacle. By June she had clearly confided this plan to 'Deborah', as she knew Juliet, for her diary states: 'We are both stark, staring, raving mad. There is definitely no doubt about it and we are both thrilled by the thought.' Later comes the entry: 'We discussed our plans for moidering (*sic*) mother.' And next day: 'We decided to use a brick in a stocking rather than a sandbag . . . Next time I write in the diary mother will be dead.'

The entry for 22 June 1954 read: 'I am writing a little of this up in the morning before the death. I felt very excited and the night before Christmassy last night. I did not have pleasant dreams though.'

That day people sitting in the tearoom in Victoria Park, Christchurch, were disturbed when the two girls crashed through the door in an excited state. 'Please help,' said one. 'Mummy's been hurt.' People enjoying a quiet day out noticed the blood stains on the girls' clothes and rushed back with them to where a woman was lying below an old wooden bridge. 'She slipped and hit her head as she bumped down the steps,' said the girls.

The woman's head was lying in a little pool of blood, and the police and ambulance were called. The police immediately noticed a half-brick soaked in blood and a blood-stained stocking torn open at the foot. The woman had clearly died of multiple head injuries. At the mortuary a pathologist found bruises around her neck, and concluded she had been held by the throat and repeatedly struck on the head. There were 45 injuries, coincidentally one for each year of her life.

It did not take detectives long to extract a confession from Pauline. However, she was completely composed, and insisted that Juliet, who had walked on ahead, had not been a party to the attack and had not suspected that it would happen. Juliet, who had earlier concurred in the story of Mrs Rieper falling from the bridge, now changed her account and, surprisingly, it tallied with Pauline's . . . she had walked

The spot where Honora Rieper was murdered.

Above
The crowd outside the courthouse where the two girls were charged with murder.
Below
A headline from a contemporary New Zealand newspaper, reflecting the interest aroused by the case.

ahead and returned to find the scene as described. Police had caught Pauline at the police station trying to burn a note meant for Juliet reading: 'I am taking the blame for everything', so perhaps this was a contingency story previously agreed between them.

After arresting Pauline, however, police found her diary, which so incriminated Juliet in the plot that the latter now had to confess her part. She admitted she had walked ahead a little and had dropped on the path a pink stone of such unusual colour that Mrs Rieper would be certain to stoop to look at it or pick it up. That was the opportunity for Pauline to hit her with the half-brick contained in the stocking. Juliet

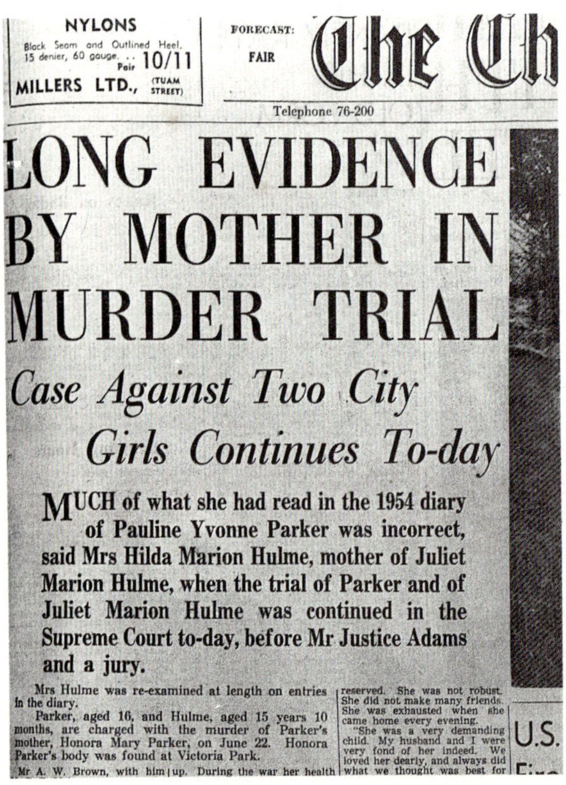

NYLONS
Black Seam and Outlined Heel. 15 denier, 60 gauge. .. Pair 10/11
MILLERS LTD., (TUAM STREET)

FORECAST: FAIR

The Ch

Telephone 76-200

LONG EVIDENCE BY MOTHER IN MURDER TRIAL

Case Against Two City Girls Continues To-day

MUCH of what she had read in the 1954 diary of Pauline Yvonne Parker was incorrect, said Mrs Hilda Marion Hulme, mother of Juliet Marion Hulme, when the trial of Parker and of Juliet Marion Hulme was continued in the Supreme Court to-day, before Mr Justice Adams and a jury.

Mrs Hulme was re-examined at length on entries in the diary.

Parker, aged 16, and Hulme, aged 15 years 10 months, are charged with the murder of Parker's mother, Honora Mary Parker, on June 22. Honora Parker's body was found at Victoria Park.

Mr A. W. Brown, with him | up. During the war her health reserved. She was not robust. She did not make many friends. She was exhausted when she came home every evening.

"She was a very demanding child. My husband and I were very fond of her indeed. We loved her dearly, and always did what we thought was best for

U.S.

claimed that, beforehand, she did not know for sure what would happen in the park, but when she turned round after Pauline delivered the first blow she knew they would have to go through with it, and that she too had taken the brick to hit Mrs Rieper. Juliet said she was terrified. The force of the blows caused the brick to burst the stocking and fall out.

Both girls were charged with murder, and the trial centred on the question of their sanity. Even after admitting the crime they remained cool and arrogant. They were incredibly rude to examining psychiatrists, Juliet further asserting that they were geniuses and above the law. In this respect there were similarities to the case of the super-intelligent Leopold and Loeb. Dr Reginald Medlicott, who appeared for the defence, found what many mothers see in a less pronounced and usually harmless way in 'difficult' children – 'a gross reversal of moral sense'. The girls admired evil and were contemptuous of things which normal people regard as decent or good.

The insanity plea was based on paranoia. They appeared normal, but in fact the killing could be regarded as proof of their condition. When the paranoic is threatened, as these girls were by what they most feared, separation, he or she becomes dangerous. Any action which removes the threat is legitimate, and even while on trial the two girls thought the killing of Mrs Rieper quite justified.

They knew that what they were doing was against the law and would be condemned by society, but these facts would not matter to them, because what they did was not an infringement of their own moral code. The law of the land was not their affair. . . .

The insanity plea failed, simply because they clearly knew that what they were doing was wrong in the eyes of the law. They were ordered to be detained during 'her majesty's pleasure.'

Although their crime was a callous one, it was possible to feel sympathy for these sad young women who might have been quite different in another environment. Mercifully, they were released in 1958.

THE LAST WOMAN HANGED IN BRITAIN

Easter cheer in a Hampstead pub – but on the street outside a jealous blonde was approaching with a gun.

Ruth Ellis with David Blakely, the man she later killed.

The name of Ruth Ellis is famous in British crime, for she was the last woman to be hanged in Britain. Her execution provoked intense debate about the desirability of capital punishment in general and for women in particular, and ten years later capital punishment for murder was abolished.

The furore overshadowed Ruth Ellis' actual crime, the final act of a sordid tale of jealousy in London's clubland. How it came about was described in a composed manner by Ruth herself at her trial.

She was born Ruth Neilson in Rhyl, a Welsh seaside resort, in 1926. She came to London, found jobs as a waitress and in a factory, and then drifted into prostitution, also working as a hostess in clubs. The embarrassment of the birth of a son by a Canadian serviceman when she was still only 18 led her later on to seek marriage, and in 1950 she became the wife of George Ellis, a dental surgeon and divorcee. They lived together for only a year, time enough for Ruth to have a daughter. She did better in business than in marriage, however, becoming the manageress of the Little Club in the well-to-do London area of Knightsbridge.

Still young and with the sort of obvious blonde good looks that go well with a darkened upstairs bar, she was an asset to the club. On top of her salary of £15 a week she had £10 a week to entertain – money with which she could give occasional treats to the tired businessmen and young blades who used the club, thus encouraging them to return. She was also given a self-contained apartment rent-free and, outside the business hours of 3 o'clock in the afternoon to 11 at night, she could use these premises to provide favours for chosen clients and increase further her income.

In 1953 she began a romance with one of the club's new members, David Blakely, a man three years her junior. He was a weak character, but had a certain amount of 'little boy lost' charm. He came from a completely different social background, had, the year before, inherited £7,000 on the death of his father, a doctor, and was indulging a desire to become a racing driver. He took part in a number of races, but with little success.

When he first met Ruth, Blakely was

The Magdala Tavern, where the shooting took place.

engaged but, according to her, she soon became pregnant by him and he offered to marry her. She obtained an abortion instead. Nevertheless, Blakely moved into her apartment.

Neither seemed to get much fulfilment from the other, and the relationship varied considerably in intensity. Ruth was also enjoying a more than casual affair with another customer of the club, a company director. Although unaware of this liaison, Blakely became jealous at his mistress's apparent cooling-off until, in 1955, she appeased him by moving in with him in a bedsitting room at 44 Egerton Gardens, Kensington. She herself had found the place, which was in the name of Mr and Mrs Ellis, and was borrowing from her other lover to pay the rent.

Ruth moved her son, now aged 10, into the cramped accommodation, became pregnant again and underwent another abortion. The claustrophobic atmosphere began to get too much for Blakely, whose usual heavy drinking increased, and the two had frequent fights and reconciliations.

The climax to their affair came when Blakely admitted his unhappiness to some married friends, Carole and Anthony Findlater. The Findlaters offered to put him up for a while in their flat at Tansa Road, Hampstead.

When Blakely failed to appear that night (it was Good Friday), Ruth rang the Findlaters and asked if he was there. She was told no, but was suspicious and called round at the flat. She found Blakely's converted van outside. When nobody answered the doorbell she pushed in the windows of the van. Anthony Findlater, having already summoned the police, went to the door and told Ruth that Blakely was not there. She did not believe him and spent most of the night spying on the flat. Next morning she saw Findlater and Blakely emerge and drive off in the damaged van.

The deception began to foster an intense jealousy in Ruth. On Saturday she left her son at the zoo and asked her second lover to drive her around to look for Blakely. One spot they tried was the Magdala public house in South Hill Park, Hampstead, near the Findlaters' flat, which was a favourite haunt of the whole set. They were unsuccessful, and in the evening Ruth was again standing in doorways, spying on the Findlaters' flat. She fancied Blakely was embarking on an affair with the Findlaters' nanny. The sounds of jollity from behind the curtains preyed upon the mind of the woman keeping her lonely vigil and made her resentment unbearable.

On Easter Sunday in the evening Ruth returned again to keep watch, but the van was not there. She assumed it would be at the Magdala, and began to walk there. She was right.

Two witnesses, Clive Gunnell (left) and Anthony Findlater, a friend of Blakely.

The others had earlier been having a party at the Findlaters' flat after a friend, Clive Gunnell, a car salesman, had arrived with his record player. About 9 o'clock, just before Ruth appeared, Gunnell and Blakely had driven off to the Magdala for fresh supplies of beer. Blakely had asked the landlord to cash a cheque, had had a drink and was emerging with his friend, three quarts of beer in his arms, when Ruth arrived, walking down the road.

Neither man saw her approach, nor did Blakely reply when she called his name. Finally, as Blakely searched his pockets for the keys to the van while trying not to drop his bottles of beer, she arrived beside him. He looked up to see her open her handbag and take out a heavy revolver – a Smith and Wesson .38. As she raised the awkward

Right
A letter by Ruth Ellis written while awaiting execution in Holloway prison.
Below
A newspaper headline stressing the intense debate about capital punishment which followed the hanging of Ruth Ellis.

weapon Blakely tried to get round the back of the van, but two shots threw him into its side. The beer bottles crashed into the road, and he called his friend's name as he staggered towards him. 'Get out of the way, Clive,' said Ruth, and followed Blakely, firing at him until he fell into the gutter, his blood mingling with the beer.

Ruth Ellis, immaculately dressed, then stood against the pub wall until an off-duty policeman took the gun from her hand and arrested her.

At her trial at the Old Bailey she admitted she had intended to kill Blakely, leaving no room for any other verdict but

Daily Mirror THURS JULY 14 1955
1½d FORWARD WITH THE PEOPLE No. 16,046

Millions of people are worried about the fate of RUTH ELLIS. Today we ask our readers—

SHOULD HANGING BE STOPPED?

RUTH ELLIS . . . HER EXECUTION HAS SET THE WHOLE WORLD TALKING.

YESTERDAY was not a happy day in Britain. The sun shone but the nation was upset.

At 9 a.m. in Holloway Gaol a woman of twenty-eight suffered death by hanging. Her body was later buried within the precincts of the prison.

Mrs. Ruth Ellis was not a virtuous woman. She admitted shooting one of her two lovers because she thought he was unfaithful. This was the gruesome end to a sordid affair.

Yet who in Britain yesterday felt happy that this mother of two children should lose her life—even though she herself had taken life?

Do the people of Britain believe that the punishment for murder should be CAPITAL PUNISHMENT?

M.P.s would not go past the prison

Are Members of Parliament satisfied that hanging is the expression of the public will?

Some M.P.s were NOT happy yesterday. Some who were to drive past Holloway Gaol on their way to the House of Commons took a different route to avoid the prison.

Five months ago M.P.s debated capital punishment. On a free vote they decided against a suggestion that the death penalty should be suspended FOR AN EXPERIMENTAL PERIOD OF FIVE YEARS and replaced by life imprisonment.

But did this vote mean that the majority of M.P.s were in favour of hanging? They voted against its suspension — not against its abolition

One man had to decide her fate

How would they have voted on the straight question: **Should we abolish the death penalty for good?**

How would they vote today?

Because there is a death sentence, one man has a terrible responsibility. In court the witnesses give evidence, the jury return a verdict, the judge passes sentence. They all represent the public conscience. All did their duty at the trial of Ruth Ellis

But one man—a professional politician who happens to be Home Secretary—had to decide whether this woman should be reprieved.

What an unenviable task

While this young woman waited in her prison cell one man had to decide whether there should be visited on her the retribution prescribed in a pitiless Biblical phrase:

"And thine eye shall not pity; but life shall go for life, eye for eye, tooth for tooth, hand for hand, foot for foot."

These words from the Old Testament Book of Deuteronomy were written probably 2,500 years ago, before the birth of Christ, by an unknown Jewish scribe

And the enlightened British nation today still follows the teaching of all those centuries ago.

It is understandable why people in Britain felt uneasy yesterday. In the rush of life the particular case of Ruth Ellis will be forgotten. But the problem of capital punishment remains

Some murderers attract much public sympathy. There has been more talk about the fate of PRETTY YOUNG Ruth Ellis than there was about the similar fate of UGLY Mrs. Christofi, aged fifty-three, who strangled her daughter-in-law.

But is it unnatural if the execution of a pretty young mother causes public distress?

One fact remains:

Whether a murderess is pretty or ugly.

Whether a murderer is young or old.

Whether a killer attracts public sympathy or not—the lawful penalty is death by hanging

Time for a change in the Law?

What the Ruth Ellis case has done is to focus attention on the whole problem of capital punishment

People are asking:

Is hanging degrading to a civilised nation? Has the time come for hanging to be abolished in Britain?

or—

Should hanging be retained as the just penalty for taking life?

The "Mirror" believes that the public should be able to voice its views.

Today we ask readers to give their verdict. There is a voting form in the Back Page.

Please express your opinion on the voting form in the Back Page

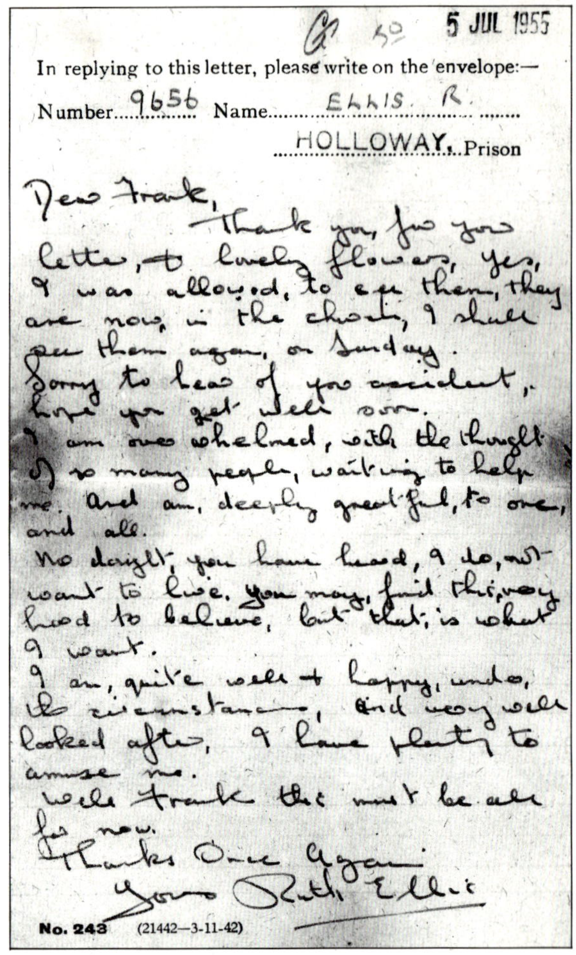
5 JUL 1955

In replying to this letter, please write on the envelope:—

Number 9656 Name ELLIS R.

HOLLOWAY Prison

Dear Frank,

Thank you, for your letter, & lovely flowers, yes, I was allowed, to see them, they are now, in the chapel, I shall see them again, on Sunday.

Sorry to hear of your accident, hope you get well soon.

I am overwhelmed, with the thought of so many people, waiting to help me. And am, deeply greatful, to one, and all.

No doubt, you have heard, I do, not want to live. You may, find this, very hard to believe, but that, is what I want.

I am, quite well & happy, under, the circumstances, and very well looked after, I have plenty to amuse me.

Well Frank this must be all for now.

Thanks Once Again.

Yours Ruth Ellis

No. 243 (21442—3-11-42)

guilty of murder or for any other penalty but hanging. The British public was not keen on the prospect of a woman being hanged and huge petitions were organized for a reprieve. But on 13 July 1955 the execution was carried out at Holloway and made legal history. All associated with Ruth Ellis's final days were impressed by her dignity – a quality she had rarely brought to her life.

How could Ruth Ellis have been so proficient with such a heavy gun and how had she obtained it? Just before her execution she claimed to her lawyers that the loaded gun had been given to her by her jealous lover, who had also driven her to Hampstead that day. The story was passed to the Home Office in a last bid for a reprieve but, since the man in question could not be found to corroborate the story, the plea failed. Later he denied that he had given her the gun. Some lawyers believe that, had the presence of such an accomplice been put forward in evidence at her trial, she might have escaped the death sentence – and her posthumous fame.

A WELL-PLANNED MILLION DOLLAR JOB

Things went as smoothly as clockwork until 'Specs' found he wasn't getting his share of the spoils.

The perfect bank robbery can be achieved. Some feature films – like the French *Rififi* – show how to carry out a perfect robbery, and to watch it planned, organized and performed is good entertainment. If nobody gets hurt it is difficult not to have a sneaking admiration for the thieves, either fictional or real, and, in fact, 11 men pulled off a brilliant robbery in Boston, Massachusetts, in 1950. Although all were known criminals, they could and should have got away with it completely. However, if there is honour among thieves, it was not in this instance the sort of honour to resist the temptation of even more money, and 11 days before the gang would have been safe, one, who had been cheated, 'blew the whistle' on the others.

The two brains behind the plan were a hoodlum of Sicilian parentage, Anthony 'Fats' Pino, and Joseph 'Big Joe' McGinnis, the son of a policeman, but an ex-convict

A detective (right) surveys the scene of the robbery.

who had served terms for theft, burglary and narcotics offences and who operated a night club in Boston. This club was near an office of Brinks Incorporated, the armoured car express company, which moved huge amounts of money around the United States with maximum security. Naturally much of this money would be stored in its vaults on any particular night, and it was this office which Pino and McGinnis planned to rob.

Other crooks were enlisted, including Joseph 'Specs' O'Keefe, a man with nearly 100 arrests to his credit, and Stanley Albert 'Gus' Gusciora. These two visited the US Patent Office in Washington to try to dis-

Left
A crowd gathers around an abandoned getaway car.

cover the specifications of the Brinks vault, but had little luck.

Despite this setback, the gang worked out every move meticulously, using plans and getaway charts and studying the habits of the employees. The big break they required was the discovery one night by O'Keefe and Gusciora that the Brinks garage attached to the building could be easily broken into. Once inside they found that they could, at their leisure, open the communicating door into the Brinks office itself. Moreover, there was nothing to prevent them reaching the vault, which was guarded by an alarm system.

With access to the bank thus secured, the gang could plan even further ahead, and the next moves were simple. They actually spent 27 nights inside the building, and on separate occasions removed the cylinders from the locks of the bank's narrow outside door giving on to Prince Street and from the four supposedly burglar-proof doors between the outside door and the vault. Each of these cylinders was taken one at a time to a locksmith who was able to make duplicate keys. The cylinders were then replaced, as good as new, in the locks at Brinks before the staff arrived in the morning.

By watching carefully the gang had discovered that the cashiers in the vault left about 7.30 in the evening, at which time they would set the alarm system. The gang's plan, therefore, was to enter the bank with their duplicate keys while only the cashiers were working in the vault, surprise them, take the money, which would be there and calmly walk out again.

The night of 17 January 1950 was chosen for the robbery, the gang making four dummy runs in the preceding weeks to test their getaway plan. There were now 11 men involved in the operation, each with a well-defined job.

On a roof opposite the building was Vincent Costa, the brother-in-law of Anthony Pino. He was the lookout man, ready to flash a light to give the break-in gang the all-clear. He would then go to street level where he would continue to keep watch in a stolen car. Outside the bank in a Ford truck, also stolen, were Anthony Pino and Joseph Banfield, ready to carry away the break-in gang and their spoils. Costa, in the lookout car, would follow the getaway truck and be ready if necessary to block any attempt at pursuit. McGinnis was to establish a firm alibi for himself and then join the gang later for the shareout. His task was to get rid of the truck and clothing and other identifiable objects after the break-in gang had dispersed.

The other seven members of the gang made the entry. They were 'Specs' O'Keefe, 'Gus' Gusciora, Henry Baker, Adolph 'Jazz' Maffie, James Faherty, Michael Geagan and Thomas F. Richardson. They wore chauffeur's caps, navy-blue jackets and grey trousers, looking very like Brinks men in these outfits. They also wore crepe-soled shoes for silence, gloves so as not to leave fingerprints and face-masks so as not to be recognized.

Around 7 pm the men walked boldly up to the bank door in Prince Street, and 'Specs' opened it without hurrying. Luckily for them it was a drizzly cold evening and nobody paid any attention.

The four internal doors were safely and silently negotiated and, within a minute or two, the five cashiers in the vault, who were counting the money to be stored overnight, looked up to discover that on the other side of the wire mesh were seven men pointing pistols at them. Although guns were stored in the vault, it would have been suicidal for anyone to attempt to reach for them, and one cashier was obliged to open the wire gate and let the gangsters in. The Brinks men were made to lie on the floor and their arms were tied with their hands behind them. Their ankles were also tied and adhesive tape was stuck across their mouths. The gang blew open a safe door with an anti-tank gun and stuffed into Brinks money bags all they could grab. Twenty minutes or so later they were walking out with $1,218,211.29 in banknotes and coins and $1,557,183.83 in securities and cheques. The alarm was raised – at 7.27 pm by a cashier who wriggled free from his rope, but by then the truck was well on its way to the house of 'Jazz' Maffie's parents – immigrants who would not understand what was going on.

The gang sorted out their loot, deciding to burn nearly $100,000 in new, traceable notes and over $1 million in other unconvertible items such as war veteran's cheques. However, the theft of these made the robbery a federal offence, which meant the FBI would be looking for them. Each gang member received $100,000 as his share of the proceeds.

All the gang were quickly rounded up by the police as part of their routine interviewing of all possible suspects, but there was no hard evidence against them. However, the seeds of their downfall were even now being sown. O'Keefe had left his share with McGinnis, and when he got it back it was down to $98,000. He gave $93,000 of this to Maffie and went to Pennsylvania with Gusciora. They stole guns for armed robberies but were quickly arrested and sent to prison, O'Keefe for three years and Gusciora for from five to twenty. While in jail they were forced, together with other members of the gang, to appear before a grand jury in Boston. The police had found some of the equipment used in the Brinks robbery and had reason to connect the gang with it. However, the jury decided there was not enough evidence to send them for trial.

When in 1954 O'Keefe was released from prison in Pennsylvania he returned to

Right
The rear doorway to the Brinks building, through which the robbers made their entrance.

A general view of the Brinks building.

Boston for his money. However, he found his $93,000 had now vanished and suspected that the gang were squeezing him out of his share. He kidnapped Costa and tried to extract his $93,000 as a ransom from Pino, but Pino bought his brother-in-law back for a 'down payment' and then engaged a New York killer, Elmer 'Trigger' Burke, to dispose of O'Keefe. O'Keefe's car was sprayed with machine gun bullets, but he was only slightly injured, and escaped further attempts on his life by getting another jail sentence for an earlier offence. Burke was to be executed in 1958 for a more successful operation.

The case was by now outside the jurisdiction of the FBI (the federal offences had a three-year statute of limitations), but until 17 January 1956 the gang were not safe from trial in Massachusetts. O'Keefe made it known that if his money was not paid over to him he would talk. Soon after Christmas 1955 FBI agents called on O'Keefe at Hampden County Jail, Springfield, Massachusetts, and informed him of the good life that Pino, Costa and McGinnis were living on the proceeds of the robbery. On 6 January 1956 O'Keefe gave the district attorney the full details of the operation.

All the gang were arrested, except Banfield, who had since died of natural causes. Gusciora broke down at the news of his friend's treachery and he, too, died before the trial, of a brain tumour.

The other eight members of the gang were tried with O'Keefe and all eight were sentenced to life imprisonment. On the plea of the district attorney, the informer, O'Keefe, was released in 1960, to go immediately into hiding, 'a sitting duck for murder' as the district attorney said. Very little of the money was ever recovered, but it had not done the gang much good. It was a perfect robbery until the robbers could not resist robbing one another.

317
MICIDE & ROBBERY

The 1960s

**A sleepwalking killer,
a great train robbery,
a horrifying tape,
a perverted strangler,
two assassinations and
a murderous 'family'.**

A Dallas policeman holds aloft the weapon used to assassinate President Kennedy.

HE KILLED WHILE ASLEEP

A New Year's drink led to death for a pretty girl – and an unusual defence for her killer.

Willis Boshears after his arrest.

It is claimed that a person cannot be hypnotized to commit a crime which he or she would be incapable of performing if not under hypnosis. But what about sleepwalkers? Sleepwalkers are known to do things of which, afterwards, they are unaware. Does their unconscious mind in any way affect their actions while sleepwalking? A sleepwalker does not walk like a zombie with arms outstretched before him, as popular myth suggests. Sleepwalkers can perform complicated acts. Could murder be one? The law has occasionally had to test cases in which the defence was that of sleepwalking, or somnambulism. If somnambulism is established, the defence is usually successful, since a sleepwalker cannot have a conscious purpose.

A Korean war hero, US Staff Sergeant Willis Eugene Boshears, claimed somnambulism as a defence when charged with the murder of a beautiful 20-year-old English girl, Jean Constable, at Dunmow, Essex, on New Year's Day, 1961.

The 29-year-old Boshears was stationed at the Wethersfield US Air Force Base, where he was serving his second three-year tour of Britain. He was happily married to a Scottish woman and they had three children, the youngest born only three weeks before. Mrs Jean Boshears had gone with the older children to her parents' home in Ayr, Scotland, for the birth, and was still there on 31 December, leaving Boshears alone on this festive night.

He had been to the club at his base and had drunk some vodka, but he still felt lonely, and in the evening he joined the local folk drinking in the public houses. In

Jean Constable, whom Boshears was accused of murdering.

one, the Bell Hotel, he met Jean Constable, from Halstead. She was a girl who liked American servicemen and was disposed to be friendly with anybody who could get her entry to the dances at Wethersfield. Boshears had in fact made her acquaintance three months earlier.

Jean had been unsuccessful in her attempts to find someone to take her to Wethersfield on this New Year's night, however, and was forced to seek her fun in the public houses. Earlier, in the Nags Head, she had made the acquaintance of 20-year-old David Sault, who was with her when she met Boshears.

The GI and the two English people spent some of the evening drinking and then, at Boshears' suggestion, went off to his flat for more drinking and dancing. The noise they made brought complaints from the neighbours both above and below. The English pair enjoyed themselves and, on a couple of occasions, when Boshears disappeared for a short while, made love.

After 'seeing in' the New Year, they agreed to stay the rest of the night with Boshears, who brought a mattress and some blankets into the sitting room, where there was a fire. Jean undressed and soon went to sleep on the mattress, where Sault joined her, while Boshears settled down on the blankets. After a little while Sault changed his mind about staying and went home. What actually happened next was

Right
Police officers at the spot where Jean Constable's body was dumped.
Below right (*inset*) David Sault, who was with Jean Constable in Boshears' flat on the night of the murder.

the question at the heart of Boshears' trial for murder.

On 3 January 1961 Jean's body was found about five miles away at Ridgewell in a water-filled ditch which ran through a field just off a 'lovers' lane'. As her liking for the American base and its occupants was known, investigation headquarters were set up there, and the US Air Force police were asked to help with enquiries. Shortly afterwards Boshears was taken to Braintree police station and charged with murder. His wife, watching the television news in Scotland, saw this short man (Boshears was known as 'Little Mac') taken from Wethersfield base with his head covered without realizing that it was her husband.

The US Air Force wanted to try Boshears, but the British authorities would not allow it, and the trial took place under British law at Essex Assizes, Chelmsford.

What happened in the fatal first hour or so of 1961? The wife of a US Air Force sergeant, in the flat above Boshears', heard a girl talking and sobbing at around 1 am. Boshears, who at first informed the police that both the girl and Sault had left together, told a different story at the trial. When Sault left, he said, he lay down beside Jean, and the next thing he remembered was a scratching and pulling at his mouth. He opened his eyes to find Jean below him dead, his hands round her throat.

In other words, Boshears was 'sleepwalking' when he killed her. At the same time he was claiming to be drunk as well as terrified and to be acting in a confused manner. He cut off Jean's hair so that she would not be recognized and burnt it. He took the body to the bathroom, washed it, dressed it as best he could, and put it on the floor of the spare bedroom. He tidied the sitting room and went back to sleep on the mattress.

When he awoke he half-remembered what had happened but thought it had been a dream. Then he discovered the body and was scared. In order to destroy evidence of the 'crime' he cleaned up the sheets, burnt Jean's fur coat and got rid of other identifying objects such as her handbag and watch. The body lay for two days

in his flat before, around midnight on 2 January, he dumped it, only for it to be discovered the next day.

At the trial Dr Francis Camps, the pathologist, said that it was improbable that Boshears could have killed Jean as he described while asleep, but would not go so far as to say that it was impossible.

The verdict hung on this point. Mr Justice Glyn-Jones' short summing up pointed out that the only two possible verdicts were 'guilty' or 'not guilty' – there were no halfway alternatives. The trend of his remarks seemed not to be in favour of the accused, but the judge had to say that if

the jury were in any doubt about whether Boshears was asleep or not, he was entitled to the benefit of it. After one hour and 50 minutes the jury gave him that benefit and he was declared 'not guilty'.

It was not a popular verdict, and there were shouts and boos when Boshears left the court. He, of course, was delighted with British justice. His wife stood by him and they went on holiday before he returned to the United States, where he was dismissed from the service.

Boshears seen with his wife on their wedding day.

THE GREAT TRAIN ROBBERY

They stole over £2 million, but their fame proved more lasting than their share of the profits.

Until 1963 'the great train robbery' would bring to mind one of the first successes of the moving picture industry: it was almost the first silent film to make any great impact on the public and was the sensation of 1903. Sixty years later a gang of at least 15 masked men succeeded in getting away with over £2½ million in a daring robbery on a train. It was called the 'crime of the century', but eventually stole from the old silent film its title. From then on 'the great train robbery' meant only one thing.

It all began in January 1963 when a gang of thieves who had recently brought off a successful airport robbery were informed of a promising railway job. An overnight mail train from Glasgow to London carried surplus money collected from banks along the route to London. The money was carried in an HVP (high value package) coach, which was always the second coach back from the diesel engine. After an August bank holiday, the gang were told, there could be as many as 250 sacks of money on the train, holding perhaps £5 million. The information came from a dishonest managing clerk of a company of solicitors, Brian Field, who had helped some of the gang before with court defences. He was a man the gang could rely upon, and they decided to attempt the big robbery.

Among their members were the following. Buster Edwards was a former small-time thief from around the Elephant and Castle district of south London, rapidly climbing the ladder into the big-time. Gordon Goody, ostensibly a hairdresser from Putney, south London, was a thief and a big, strong 'muscle-man' who usually liked

An aerial view of Leatherslade Farm, the train robbers' hideout.

to work on his own. Charlie Wilson was another big man, from Clapham, south London, whose fronts were a greengrocery and a bookmaking business. Roy James was a silversmith and a racing driver who might have succeeded in the top rank of grand prix drivers if he had not been persuaded to drive getaway cars while waiting for his opportunity. Bruce Reynolds, tall, bespectacled – a crook, like the rest, from south London – was, however, a man who, unlike the others, scorned the usual pubs and clubs, preferring to be seen in the best hotels, like the Ritz, with a pretty woman.

Early in their discussions the gang realized that for such a job, requiring precision planning, they needed an expert on railways – particularly railway robbery – and Edwards knew of just such a person, a man who had been making a living from his knowledge of the procedure by which parcels were sent by rail. His name was Roger Cordrey and he lived at East Molesey in Surrey, owning a florist's shop, which gave him a respectable front. He was approached and agreed to join the team, provided his own associates could be brought in, among them Thomas Wisbey, a London betting shop manager, and Bob Welch, who ran a club at which some of these underworld characters met.

As plans developed the gang saw that they would need a man who could actually drive the train once they had commandeered it. Reynolds remembered a man he had known in prison – Ronnie Biggs. Reynolds looked down upon him as an incompetent thief but he had the asset of an engine-driver friend, a man who took Biggs' son for rides in his cab. Reynolds approached Biggs, a carpenter and odd-job man living in Redhill, Surrey, and Biggs agreed to bring his friend into the operation on the condition that he himself was given a place in the gang. There were other gang members, including James Hussey, a painter and decorator and another strong man, Jimmy White, an ex-paratrooper and thief, and at least two others who remain uncaught and unknown to the general public.

The plan was to stop the train in the small hours of 8 August 1963, as it approached a place called Sears Crossing, between Linslade and Tring, about 40 miles, or half-an-hour's travelling time, from the London terminus of Euston. The gang arrived in two Land Rovers and a lorry at Bridego Bridge, half a mile or so further on than Sears Crossing. They were dressed as soldiers and pretended to be on manoeuvres, but once they had parked under the bridge, assumed blue boiler suits of the sort railway workers might wear. They also put on balaclava-type masks. Telephone lines from the bridge were cut, and a marker consisting of two metal poles dug into the ground with a piece of white cloth hung between them was placed

Right
Bruce Reynolds, one of the leading lights in the robbery.
Far right
Charles Wilson, another important member of the gang.

Far left
Roger Cordrey, whose original sentence of 20 years was later reduced.
Left
James Hussey, a painter and decorator by profession.
Below left
Thomas Wisbey, who joined the gang at a later stage.

where the train was required to stop.

Each man had his allotted task. Reynolds, with a walkie-talkie, was the lookout – he passed on the message that the train was coming. At a dwarf signal one of the gang covered the green light and switched on the warning amber light, as he had been shown by Cordrey. This told the driver that the next signal, on a gantry at Sears Crossing, might be red. Indeed it was, because Cordrey covered the green light with a glove and switched on the red. The train slowed at the first signal and stopped at the second.

Two of the gang immediately set to work uncoupling the second coach from the third. Edwards spotted the fireman coming back from the cut telephone lines at the side of the track and threw him down the embankment where two other members of the gang subdued him. The heavies now mounted the cab, where the driver, Jack Mills, tried to resist but was struck twice with a cosh, blood pouring from the wounds in his head. The driver and fireman were handcuffed together and the new driver was brought aboard, with the object of taking the engine and the mail coach containing the sacks of money further down the line to where the lorry was waiting below the bridge. The rest of the train would remain where it was. The new driver, terrified, could not get the engine to start, so the original driver was brought back and forced to move the train forward to where the white marker was showing.

Meanwhile the heavies had moved into the mail van, breaking the doors and windows with crowbars and coshes in order to gain access. Five men sorting mail were instructed to lie on the floor. The padlock of the cage holding the money sacks was smashed, a sack was opened to reveal bundles of banknotes, and the gang formed a chain and passed 120 sacks down to the lorry.

When the agreed time was up, the handcuffed driver and fireman were brought into the coach and made to lie down with the others. They were told not to move for half an hour while the gang made their escape. They left six sacks behind, together with one which they noticed they had dropped in the road as they moved off.

They took the money to Leatherslade Farm, an isolated farmhouse near the village of Oakley, about 25 miles away. They had bought the farm some days before by arrangement with Brian Field, who had acted on behalf of a client, Leonard Field (no relation). Leatherslade had workshops and garages where the lorry and Land Rovers could be hidden so as not to be visible, even from the air. As they arrived, they heard on their short-wave radio the first police message informing all cars of the train robbery.

At the farm the gang shared out the money – it came to £2,631,684 – and, after deducting the expenses, i.e. money promised to helpers and as payment for information received, the 17 full members had shares of £150,000 each, worth considerably more in 1963 than it is today.

The plan had been to lie low until the end of the week when the immediate hue and cry should have subsided, but their threat to the train crew to keep quiet for half an hour now rebounded on them. The police (quite illogically) took this to mean that the gang had a nearby hide-out, and asked all local people by radio to let them know about any suspicious sights or sounds. They also announced they would be calling at all likely hiding places within the area. This panicked the robbers into leaving earlier than they intended and before they had cleared away all traces of their use of the farm. The final tidying up had been arranged through Brian Field, but the person engaged to carry this out was too scared to go near the farm.

The robbers would have been well advised to stay until the Sunday. It was not until Monday that a curious farm labourer noticed the bonnet of the lorry and the padlocked garage. He informed the police by phone, but when by Tuesday they had not come round to investigate, he rang again. This time the police came and realized that they had found the hideaway. Mistakenly, they announced their discovery – mistakenly because James, Wilson, Edwards and Reynolds were on their way back to the farm to destroy any evidence when they heard the news.

Police found plenty of fingerprints in the farm, despite the gang's intention to wear gloves at all times and they soon knew the identities of many of the robbers.

The first to be caught was the railway expert, Roger Cordrey. He had enlisted the help of a friend, Bill Boal, to hide his share of the money, although how much Boal knew about the robbery is debatable. It is possible that he was unaware of Cordrey's involvement. The two men went to Bournemouth on the south coast, bought a car and a van, and hired two lock-up garages, intending to leave the money in the two vehicles until it was safe to use it. Unfortunately Boal paid one garage owner three months' rent in advance from a thick wad of banknotes, which was quite unnecessary and only served to make the owner, a policeman's widow, suspicious. She rang the police while the men were parking the van. They were arrested and the money was recovered.

More was recovered when a couple found three bags of money in a wood in Dorking, Surrey, and investigating police also discovered a suitcase. The bags contained £109,000 and a German boarding house receipt on which was written the name of Brian Field, the solicitor's clerk.

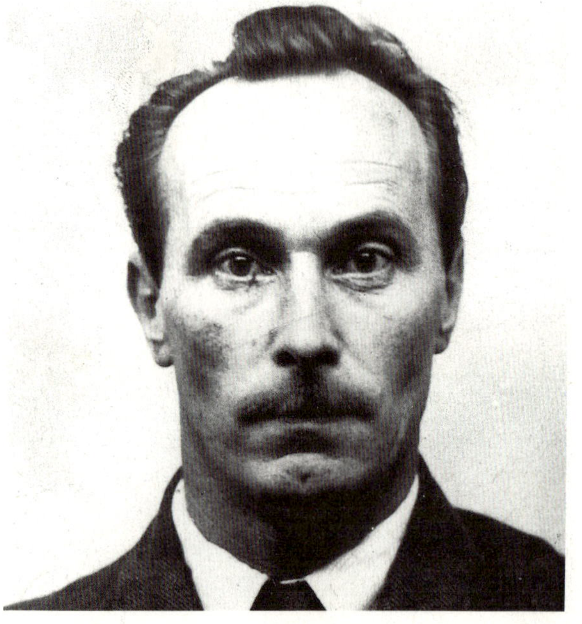

Right
Jimmy White, ex-paratrooper and thief, who left his fingerprints in a caravan.

Far left
Bill Boal, who was implicated in the robbery.
Left
Gordon Goody, another member of the south London underworld.

He had panicked and had asked a relative to throw away his share. By chance police searching the area also came across an empty caravan four miles away at Box Hill. When a panel on the wall was removed, over £30,000 in notes was found behind. Fingerprints in the van matched those of Jimmy White.

Descriptions of White, Wilson and Reynolds were released to the press and Wilson was soon picked up. Goody and Wisbey were also questioned, but not held because of lack of evidence. However, Wisbey was arrested soon after when his palm print was found to match one on a bath-rail at the farm. Biggs was arrested because his prints matched those on a plate, but he did not mention his train-driver friend. A friend of Reynolds, John Daly, was arrested, his prints being on a game of Monopoly found at the farm. The details discovered by police concerning the purchase of the farm led to the arrest of Leonard Field and the solicitor whom Brian Field worked for, John Wheater. James Hussey was pulled in, his print

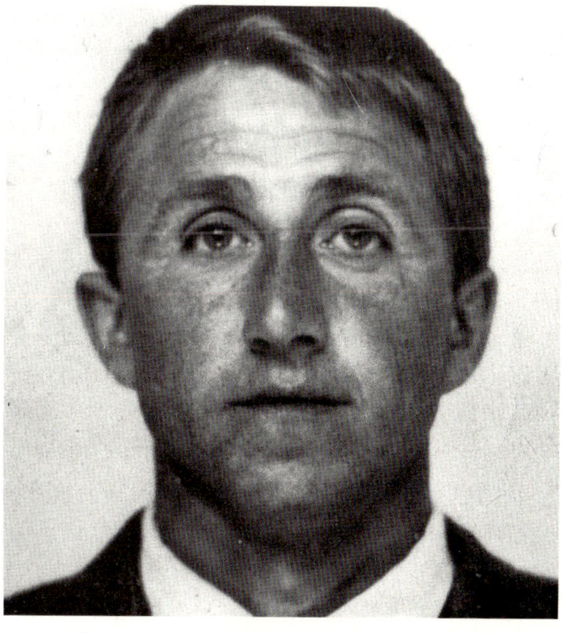

Far left
Brian Field, who helped in the purchase of Leatherslade Farm.
Left
Roy James, silversmith and racing driver.

Top right
Leonard Field, whose 25-year sentence was reduced to five years on appeal.
Centre right
John Wheater, a solicitor who was involved with the gang.
Below right
Ronald Biggs at home in Brazil with his son Michael.

having been found on the tailboard of the lorry at the farm – Hussey's velvet gloves had shrunk because of his sweat. Welch was arrested, his palm print being on a beer can.

James was arrested after a chase over roofs, since he had spotted the police arriving at his front door. He was caught with a bag holding £12,000. Goody was finally arrested through specks of paint on his shoes which matched some at the farm.

Only three robbers known to the police succeeded in evading capture. They were Buster Edwards and Bruce Reynolds, the two leading lights in the crime, who escaped abroad (they met up in Mexico) and Jimmy White. There were probably three others unknown.

The trial of the rest began at Aylesbury on 20 January 1964. Cordrey's trial was deferred, because he pleaded guilty, and Biggs' trial was halted and a retrial ordered because it inadvertently came out in evidence that he had served a prison sentence.

Daly was discharged on the orders of the judge when his counsel submitted that his prints on the Monopoly game could have got there at any time – they did not tie him unquestionably to the farm. Reynolds had always said he liked Daly because Daly seemed to be lucky.

All the others were found guilty and the sentences handed down shocked the public. Cordrey was sentenced first and received 20 years. Boal, Wilson, Wisbey, Welch, Hussey, James, Goody and Biggs were all found guilty of conspiracy and armed robbery. Boal received 24 years and the others 30 years. The two Fields received 25 years for conspiracy. Wheater received three years.

On appeal, the sentences of the two Fields were reduced from 25 to five years, the conviction for conspiracy to rob being quashed, and Cordrey and Boal had their sentences reduced from 20 and 24 to 14 years. Boal's case was a sad one – he had not even been present at the robbery. The injustice destroyed him and in 1966 he was moved to a psychiatric prison, but was then transferred to Wormwood Scrubs. He died of a brain tumour in 1970.

Left
Buster Edwards (left) at his London flower stall greets Michael Biggs.

Most of the prisoners tried to escape. Wilson was 'rescued' by friends on 12 August 1964 and made his way to France. A month later Ronnie Biggs escaped. A friend arranged the getaway by means of a pantechnicon with the roof cut away and an extendable scaffolding tower inside, which enabled him to mount the prison wall and throw down a rope. There were now five at large: Reynolds, Edwards, White, Wilson and Biggs.

In 1966 White was recognized and his whereabouts made known to the police. He was arrested and pleaded guilty. His sentence was comparatively lenient – 18 years.

Edwards and his family could not adapt to the life in Mexico and in September 1966 he returned and gave himself up – he received 15 years. Wilson went to Canada and seemed to be managing happily enough, but in January 1968 an officer from Scotland Yard arrived and he was taken back to serve his sentence.

Reynolds and his family found life in Mexico, where he could not work, expensive. He felt apprehensive in Canada, went to the south of France and then returned to London, where he began behaving recklessly as if courting arrest. He moved to Torquay in Devon, where in November 1968 he, too, was arrested. His sentence was 25 years.

Biggs, the least professional of them all as a thief, was the best organized at living while on the run. He and his wife and children went to Australia and were happy until he was nearly caught – he fled alone to Brazil. His wife stayed in Australia and made a successful life, while Biggs lived openly in Brazil, resisting all attempts to extradite him because he had become the father of a boy, whose existence gave Biggs the right to stay.

The other train robbers were gradually released, most around 1975. Welch was the last to be set free (except for Reynolds, sentenced later), on 14 June 1976. Few had any money left. 'Minders' had spent it for them and only some £400,000 was recovered. Legal fees took a lot. Some robbers, or their wives, later made money from memoirs.

The great train robbers became glamorous figures in the eyes of the public. In the late 1980s a film, *Buster*, was made of the life of Edwards, with Phil Collins playing the lead.

Against the glamour can be set the story of Jack Mills, the train driver who was coshed. He was 58 at the time, and did not work properly again. He suffered increasingly from bad health, and died less than seven years later (though not from his injuries, said the coroner). Many drew a lesson from his story and the £250 reward for bravery he received from the Post Office, comparing it with the £65,000 allegedly paid by a newspaper for the memoirs of Ronnie Biggs' wife.

Jack Mills, the driver of the hijacked train.

THE MOORS MURDERERS

They recorded their sadistic killings and photographed themselves by the moorland graves of their victims.

Of all the pieces of evidence given in British murder trials, a tape recording lasting 16 minutes and 21 seconds had the biggest effect. It branded Ian Brady and Myra Hindley as two of the most callous murderers ever brought to justice. Although in prison Hindley turned to religion, took an Open University degree in humanities and had powerful friends to support her plea that she was no longer a threat to society, the horror of that recording has meant that ordinary mercy has been denied her for over 20 years.

Brady, the illegitimate son of a Glasgow waitress, and Hindley, born during the Second World War, were both brought up in slums, but whereas Brady had always shown a cruel streak, being known as 'Dracula' in the rough Gorbals district of Glasgow where he lived as a boy, Hindley developed religious feelings and had attended the Roman Catholic church.

Their paths had crossed when they began working for the same company in Gorton, Manchester, Millwards Merchandise Ltd, which distributed chemicals – he a stock clerk and she a typist. Hindley was entranced by the good-looking, arrogant Brady, and confessed as much to her diary – congratulating herself when, towards the end of 1961, he asked her out. They discovered in each other a keen interest in Nazism – a coincidence which had terrible consequences – and went to see a film, *Judgment at Nuremberg*. Brady began explaining to Hindley some of his philosophy. He seemed to be strongly influenced by Nietzsche and his ideas of a superman, and by the Marquis de Sade, and was interested in torture and violence.

In November 1963 Hindley, then 21 (Brady was five years older), passed her driving test and began driving Brady around the Lancashire moors in her Austin Mini Traveller. It was in that month that 12-year-old John Kilbride disappeared. On Boxing Day, 1964, 10-year-old Lesley Ann Downey vanished after visiting a fairground with a young friend.

The man who was instrumental in linking the deaths of these children to Brady and Hindley was David Smith, who was married to Hindley's younger sister, Maureen. Although only 18 in 1965 Smith had a record of violence. He had fallen under Brady's influence, and had written in a notebook that murder was a hobby and a supreme pleasure.

On 6 October 1965 Hindley had visited the Smiths late, and David Smith had been asked to escort her back to 16 Wardle

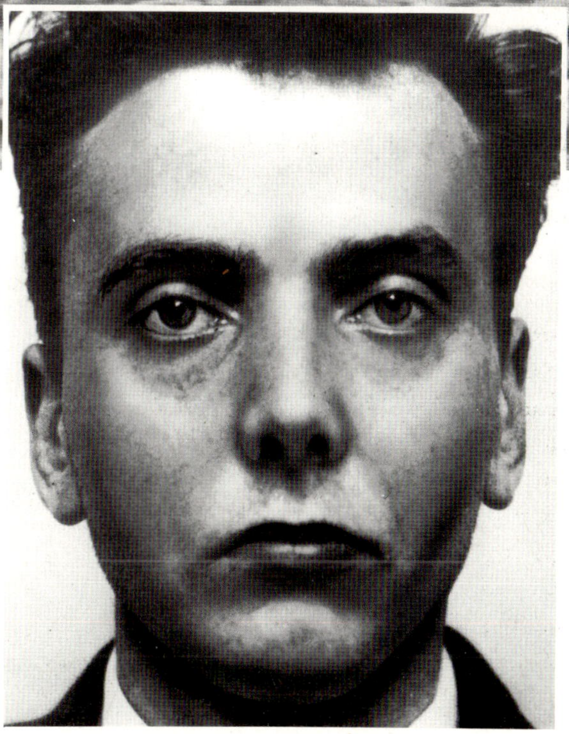

Above
Police carrying down the body of John Kilbride from the moors.
Left (*inset*)
Myra Hindley and Ian Brady.

Brook Avenue, Hattersley, Manchester, the council house in which Hindley and Brady were living with the occupier, Hindley's grandmother. Shown into the kitchen, Smith heard a terrible scream, and (as he later described it) was called from the kitchen to the living room by Hindley to help Brady. There he saw Brady throwing around what, at their trial, he said he thought was a floppy rag doll, but soon

Right
Lesley Ann Downey, whose dying screams were recorded on tape.
Below right
John Kilbride, who disappeared in November 1963

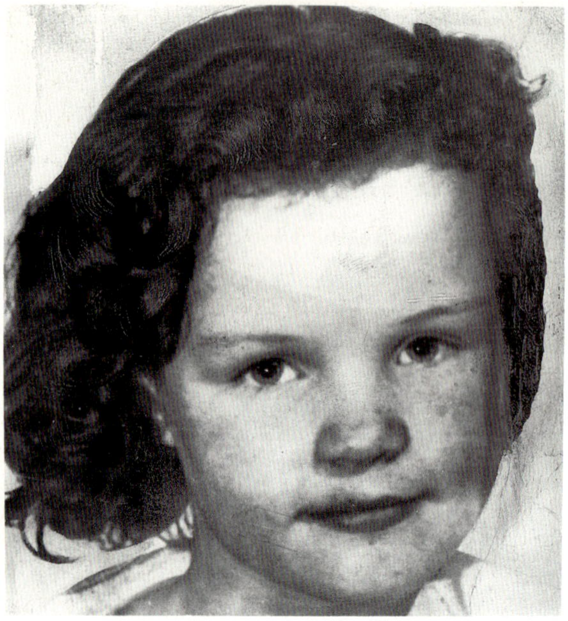

realized was a groaning boy. Brady then brought an axe down on the boy's head and did so again to try to stop the groaning. Then, when the victim made a gurgling noise, he wrapped electrical wire round his neck and pulled. He then said to Hindley: 'That's it. It's the messiest yet.'

Although Smith had discussed and even planned crimes with Brady before, this scene proved too much for him. After getting out of the house at about 3.30, he went home and told his wife what had happened. At 6.10 he and his wife rang Stalybridge police station from a call box. At 6.20 am he was picked up from the box in a terrified state by a patrol car and related his horrific story. To get into No 16 Wardle Brook Avenue, a police superintendent took the place of a bread roundsman and with white coat and basket of loaves knocked on the door.

Hindley opened it, and the police entered to witness the aftermath of the gruesome crime. Brady was on a divan writing a note to his employers telling them that because of an injured ankle (hurt in the struggle) he would not be at work that day. In reality he intended digging a grave on the moors for his victim. By now the body was tied in a crouching posture and wrapped in polythene sheeting and a blanket in a spare room, and the room of the murder had been spotlessly cleaned of all the blood that had bespattered it.

The murdered youth was 17-year-old Edward Evans, a homosexual whom, it was discovered, Brady had met at Manchester Central Station snack bar that day. But it was further discoveries in the house, and Smith's story of Hindley boasting of other hidden bodies, that set the police searching Saddleworth Moor, near Manchester. Hidden in the spine of a prayer book, *The Garden of the Soul*, given to Hindley after her first communion, were two left-luggage tickets issued at Manchester Central Station. Two suitcases were retrieved. They contained wigs, masks, photographs and tape recordings. Some photographs were of Hindley posing on the moors on what were to prove to be the graves of Lesley Ann Downey and John Kilbride. Police found them, 373 yards apart, on each side of the A635, the road taken by Hindley's car.

Hindley and Brady were charged with the three murders and their trial opened at Chester Assizes on 19 April 1966. Because of the evidence given at the committal proceedings, it provoked great public interest, and was called the 'trial of the century', although there was no doubt of the couple's guilt. They had kept photographs of their victims, who had been forced to pose in obscene positions. But it was the tape recording of the death of Leslie Ann Downey which caused the most drama. The judge pondered hard on whether it should be heard in public or not.

Although the accused were in a bulletproof dock, police feared a murder attempt as the tape was played, and formed a guard round the prisoners.

The child's voice, combining fear and desperation, was heard pleading to God and to her tormentors, asking not to be undressed, claiming she was being hurt, asking to see mummy, saying she had to be home by eight o'clock 'or she would be killed'. Then there were screams and, towards the end, bearing in mind that it was 26 December, the sound of the radio being turned on, broadcasting Christmas bells and two songs, 'Jolly St Nicholas' and 'The Little Drummer Boy'. This music was

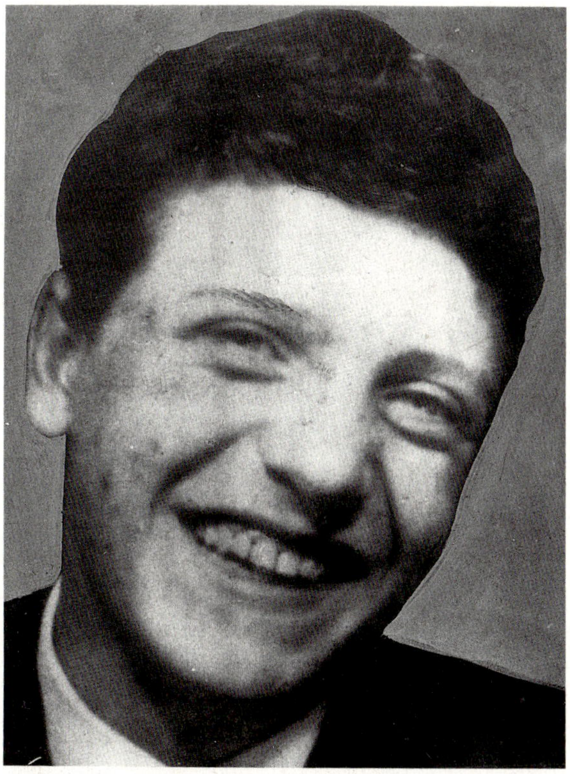

'faded in' as if the whole tape had been planned like a radio programme, to be listened to and enjoyed later. The judge had demanded silence during the playing of the tape, but many listeners could not hide their distress.

Brady was arrogant and rude during $8\frac{3}{4}$ hours in the dock, admitting the murder of Evans but denying those of the two children, and defending his perverted erotic tastes and his adulation of Adolf Hitler. Hindley, whose hair had been dyed a startling silver-lilac on the first day of the trial, gave nearly six hours of evidence on the 11th day, when her hair was a bright yellow. She was quieter, and admitted cruelty and her shame when taxed about the tape recording. However, she claimed that Lesley left the house afterwards with Smith, the main prosecution witness, and that she had not seen her again. Each of the accused had made an attempt to shift the responsibility for the crimes on to Smith.

After two hours and 20 minutes the jury found Brady guilty of three murders, and Hindley guilty of two and of harbouring Brady after the murder of John Kilbride. They escaped the death penalty since it had been abolished in Britain between the time of the crimes and the convictions. Brady was sentenced to three concurrent terms of life imprisonment (normally ten years, but with the possibility of release on licence after a third of that time with the home secretary's approval). Hindley was given two concurrent terms of life imprisonment, plus a concurrent term of seven years for being an accessory.

In 1973, only seven years after the trial, a newspaper published stories that a reformed Hindley had been taken for early morning walks in a London park, presumably prior to release. There was such a public outcry that this practice was stopped.

It was always believed that there were other victims of Brady and Hindley buried on the moors. In 1963 a 16-year-old girl, Pauline Reade, who lived two doors from David Smith and who was an acquaintance of Hindley, disappeared, and in 1964 a 11-year-old boy disappeared near where Brady lived.

In 1988 Hindley volunteered to cooperate with police in trying to find additional bodies, and was escorted to various spots, including places shown on photographs found in the suitcases, with this aim in mind. Eventually the body of Pauline Reade was discovered, but Hindley was unsuccessful in finding others. The public was horrified at this reminder of the terrible story. There was further vilification of the murderers and more opposition to the suggestion that Hindley might be released. It seems that the tape recording will never be forgotten while any are left who heard it.

Left
Edward Evans, murdered with an axe and a length of wire.

THE KILLER IN GREEN TROUSERS

A bow was his trademark, and he held a city in terror while police sought him in vain.

Nobody was ever charged with the series of sex killings which brought terror to Boston in the 1960s, but it is generally accepted that Albert De Salvo was the man who achieved worldwide notoriety as 'the Boston Strangler'.

The story begins on 14 June 1962 at 77 Gainsborough Street, Boston. Mrs Anna Slesers, a 55-year-old divorcee, was await-

ing the arrival of her son to take her to a service at the Latvian church near by. When Julius Slesers arrived, around eight o'clock, he received no answer to his knock, and was worried enough to break open the door of the third-floor apartment. He was confronted with the horrible sight of the body of his mother lying on the floor, naked except for a housecoat flung open. Her legs were spread wide, and around her neck was the blue cord from the housecoat, knotted tightly and finished with a bow beneath her chin.

A few drawers had been rummaged through and the contents of a waste bin were scattered around as if a burglar had been disturbed, but Mrs Slesers had been sexually assaulted, so the police were unsure what type of criminal they were looking for.

They had a clearer idea two weeks later when a 68-year-old widow, Mrs Nina Nichols, met her death in an apartment block in Commonwealth Avenue in a remarkably similar fashion. Mrs Nichols had been speaking on the telephone to her sister when the doorbell rang. Informing her sister of this, she promised to ring straight back when she had answered the door. She never did, nor did she arrive for dinner as arranged. Her brother-in-law rang the janitor of Mrs Nichols' block and asked him to see if Mrs Nichols was all right.

The janitor found her strangled with one of her own stockings, tied in a bow beneath her chin. She was naked, except for a housecoat pulled up above her waist. She had been sexually assaulted, and the room had been ransacked to fake a burglary, although nothing had been taken. The similarities with the case of Mrs Slesers were obvious, and the police guessed they were seeking a maniac.

From June 1962 until the beginning of 1964 13 women were killed in Boston in similar circumstances. One victim was stabbed and another died of a heart attack, presumably as a result of the sexual assault by the killer. The other 11 were strangled, usually with their stockings. The ages of the victims ranged from 19 to 85. Four were in their twenties, and one of these was strangled the day after the stunned nation had heard of President Kennedy's assassination. Her stockings were round her neck, tied in the killer's trademark, a bow. Most of the women were sexually assaulted and their bodies left in obscene positions.

The murders came to an end in January 1964, but in October of that year police in Cambridge, Massachusetts, got a good

Left
Albert De Salvo, in sailor's uniform, after his arrest.

Right and opposite **The 13 women killed by the Boston Strangler.**

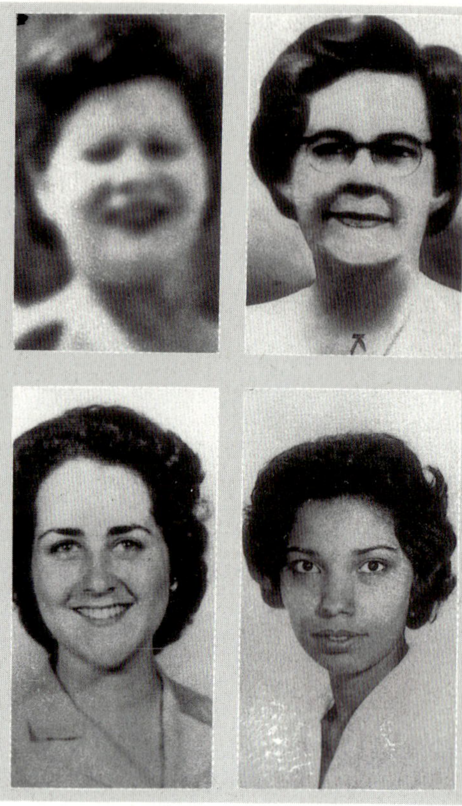

lead on another sex attacker, called 'the Green Man.' He was so nicknamed because he always wore green trousers when breaking into the homes of young women. He would force them to strip at knifepoint, and fondle and kiss them all over before departing.

On 27 October, at 9.30 am, he appeared in the bedroom of a young housewife, dozing after her husband had left for work. Threatening her with a knife, he gagged her with her underwear, and tied her to the four bedposts. After caressing and kissing her body, he loosened her bonds and fled, muttering an apology. The woman gave the police an excellent description of him, and the sketch made by a police artist was recognized by a detective 'This looks like the Measuring Man', he said.

'The Measuring Man' was Albert De Salvo, who in 1960 had been convicted of assaulting pretty women by posing as an artist's agent. Calling at their homes, he promised them employment as models and used a tape measure to measure them. In doing so he took liberties which led to complaints, conviction and several months in prison. His term of imprisonment had ended in April 1962, two months before the Boston Strangler first struck. Incredibly, throughout all the questioning of known sexual perverts that the police had routinely performed, they had missed De Salvo. Now they invited him to police headquarters and, although he denied the assault on the young women, she instantly recognized him and he was charged.

Even now there was nothing to connect him with other offences until police circulated his photograph in nearby states. Dozens of women now recognized him as 'the Green Man'.

De Salvo, born in 1931, had, after a childhood record of housebreaking, joined the US army, and married a local girl while serving in Germany. She bore him two children but divorced him, having complained of his excessive sexual demands. Before returning to the United States to become a maintenance man, he was the army's middleweight boxing champion.

While De Salvo was being questioned at Cambridge, his 30-year-old second wife urged him to tell everything, and he confessed to 400 break-ins and a couple of rapes 'you don't know about'. To enter apartments he used a strip of polyethylene which he slid into the locks to release the mechanism. De Salvo was convicted of 'the Green Man' crimes, earlier sexual offences and various robberies, and in 1967 was sentenced to life imprisonment.

Before that he had been sent to the state mental institution at Bridgewater, Massachusetts, where he convinced doctors and lawyers that he was the Boston Strangler.

As the Strangler his method was to knock on apartment doors until he received an answer when, to gain admittance, he would pretend to have been sent to do maintenance work. He described the murders in 50 hours of tape recordings, revealing details that only the Strangler could have known. He described a certain 'time' which came upon him when he had to do these things. Asked about the older, not sexually attractive victims, he said that attraction had nothing to do with it, that it was an immediate impulse.

His defence attorney, F. Lee Bailey, described De Salvo, who, as well as his green trousers, liked immaculately pressed white shirts and wore his hair slicked back

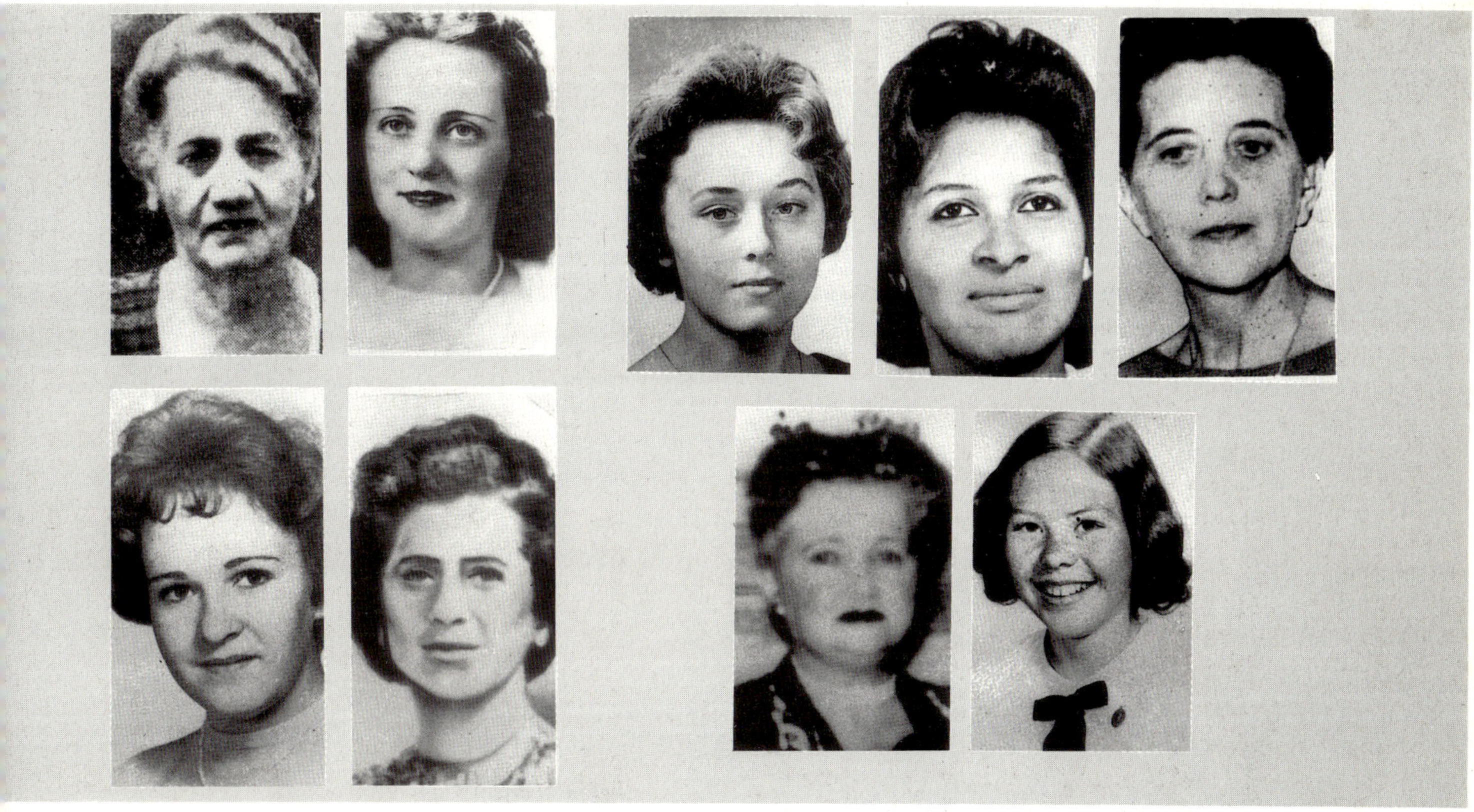

with oil, as 'a victim of one of the most crushing sexual drives that psychiatric science has ever encountered'. He further declared that his client was undoubtedly a schizophrenic, and he called him an uncontrolled vegetable in a human body.

De Salvo lived only six years in Walpole State Prison, Massachusetts. In 1973, when he was 42 years old, he was found dead in his cell from stab wounds administered by other inmates after an argument about drugs.

State troopers controlling the crowd of curious onlookers opposite the police station where De Salvo was being held.

THE SHOOTING EVERYBODY REMEMBERS

Even a judicial commission failed to find the truth when a President was shot and his assassin murdered.

Above
John F. Kennedy at the beginning of the fateful motorcade through Dallas.

Political assassinations attract clichés. 'The shot that echoed round the world' is honoured by time. The assassination of John F. Kennedy, 35th president of the United States, is an event which is said to have had such an effect on individuals that they can recall exactly where they were and what they were doing when they heard about it. The world's news services and media communications were such in 1963 that there can never before have been a story which spread so rapidly around the globe.

John Kennedy was born on 29 May 1917 in Boston, Massachusetts, the second son of very rich Irish-American parents. In a family which grew to nine children, Jack (as he was known) was for a long time overshadowed by his handsome elder brother Joe, who was better at sports and studies. Jack was, in fact, not a healthy or a particularly bright child. Both brothers served in the Second World War, Jack becoming a naval hero when his torpedo boat was sunk and his bravery and inspiration led to the rescue of his men.

He emerged from the war with a permanent back injury, but, sadly, brother Joe was killed in 1944. This tragedy coloured Jack's remaining life, for he became his ambitious father's main hope of political success. His determination and the family wealth won him rapid advancement, first

as congressman and then as senator for Massachusetts. In 1961 he was elected president.

Kennedy was only 43, the youngest US president in history and the first Roman Catholic. He had a beautiful young wife, the former Jacqueline Lee Bouvier, a three-year-old daughter and a baby son. He won the election largely by impressive television debates with his clearly less 'clean-cut' Republican opponent, Richard Nixon. Through this exposure Kennedy was as instantly recognizable to his countrymen as any American had ever been. As president, the inspiring speeches he made about the country's problems, such as

A camera captures the moment when Kennedy slumps into his wife's arms after being struck by the assassin's bullet.

poverty and the status of black people, in which he spoke of 'the New Frontier', led to a fresh, liberal and exhilarating atmosphere in the United States. His wife, whose extravagant redecoration of the White House achieved maximum publicity, helped to create the feeling that a vibrant new era was beginning.

An early setback to Kennedy's period in office was a humiliatingly abortive invasion of Communist Cuba, a plan he had inherited from the previous president, Dwight Eisenhower. However, later, in blockading Cuba and forcing the Soviet leader Nikita Khrushchev to remove missiles from that country, he scored an outstanding foreign affairs success. His stands on questions of industrial relations and civil rights had made him a popular president and, midway through his term of office, it seemed certain he would be elected again. In order to improve his standing in the southern states, where his civil rights attitudes were less popular, he and his wife set off on a fateful tour of Florida and Texas.

On 22 November 1963 Kennedy's motorcade passed through Dallas, Texas. He and Mrs Kennedy sat in the back of an open car, with the governor of Texas, John B. Connally, and his wife sitting in front of them. Large crowds gave them a warm welcome but, as the car neared the Dealey Plaza and turned left past the Texas School Book Depository, shots rang out. Kennedy clutched his neck and slumped down. He was cradled by his wife who, according to Mrs Connally, said: 'They have killed my husband . . . I have his brains in my hand'. John Connally, sitting immediately in front of Kennedy , was also hit, and was lying across his wife's lap.

The president's car sped to the Parkland Memorial Hospital in Dallas. One bullet had passed through Kennedy's neck (and, it is supposed, had then hit Connally), while another went through his head. Connally recovered, but the president had died almost immediately.

The shots were fired from the Book Depository building by 24-year-old Lee Harvey Oswald, an employee of the Depository. On the sixth floor of the building

there was found a sniper's nest, which contained the Mannlicher-Carcano rifle he had used and three spent cartridges. Oswald walked calmly from the building and went home, where he changed his clothes, picked up a pistol and returned to the streets. He was stopped by a police patrolman, J. D. Tippit, and shot him four times at point-blank range, killing him. The last shot was fired as he stood over the fallen officer. Oswald fled to the Texas Theater Cinema and went inside without paying in order to hide in the darkness. When police officers approached him, inside the cinema, he again attempted to shoot, but his pistol misfired and he was arrested after a struggle.

Oswald was born on 18 October 1939 in New Orleans. He was described as 'emotionally disturbed' at school, from which he dropped out at 16, joining the marines a year later. Subsequently discharged, he went to the Soviet Union, where he married a 19-year-old girl and obtained a residence visa. However in 1962 he was

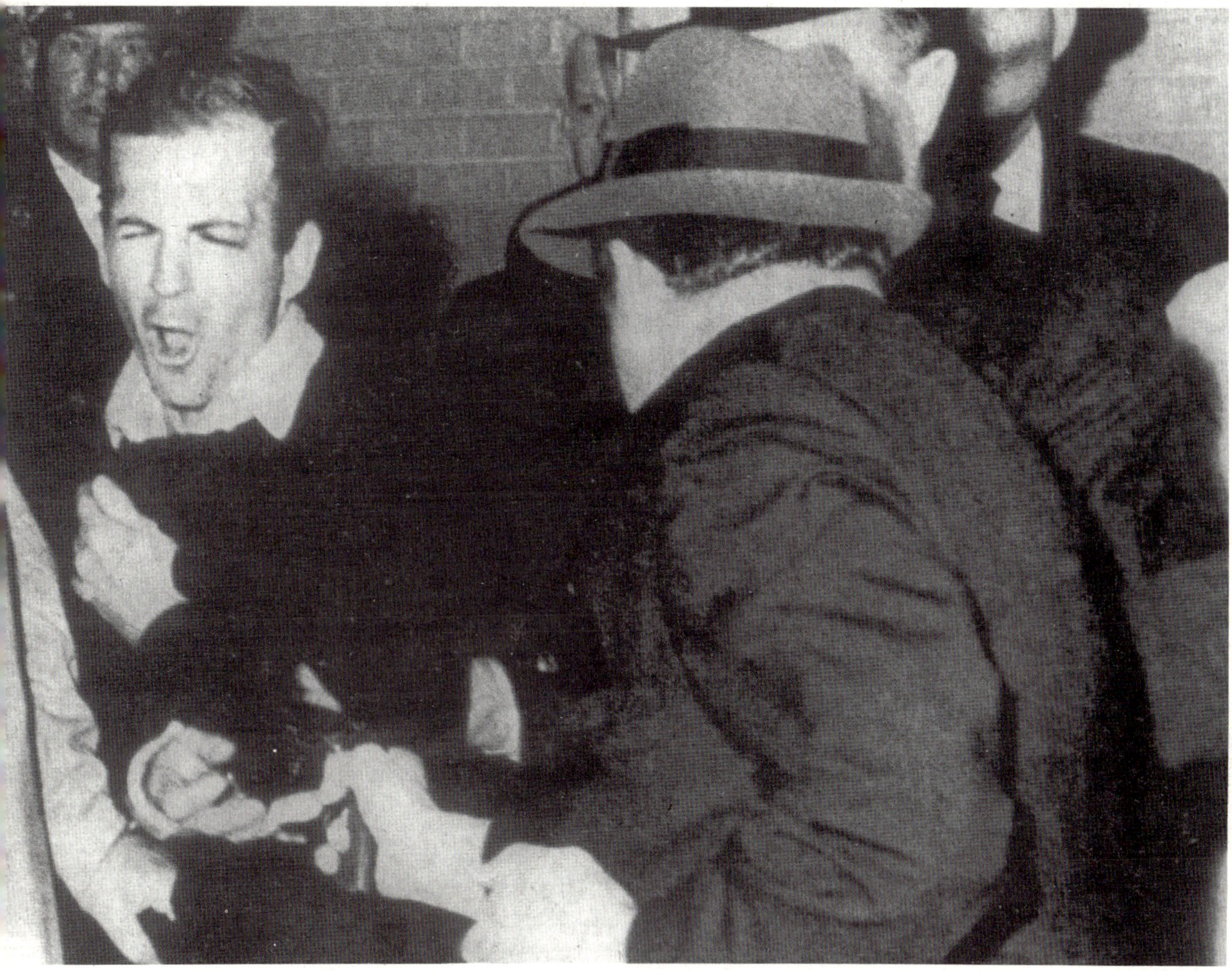

Lee Harvey Oswald's face is contorted in agony as Jack Ruby fires.

told he could stay no longer. He attempted suicide before leaving with his wife and daughter for the United States.

In March 1963, while living in Dallas, Oswald bought the assassination weapon by mail order. His wife later stated that he used the rifle in an abortive attempt to kill a retired US army general. Oswald tried to return to the Soviet Union and also attempted to get to Cuba, but failed. His wife and two daughters were by now living with friends, where they were visited by Oswald the day before Kennedy was shot.

Oswald, a confused individual with fluctuating communist sympathies, had links with both extreme left-wing and right-wing organizations, and his political stance has defied coherent retrospective analysis. Two days after his arrest, he was being transferred to the county jail, an operation being watched by millions on television, when a 52-year-old night-club operator, Jacob Rubenstein, better known as Jack Ruby, stepped forward and shot him dead as he was held by police officers. Ruby was described as a man overcome by the killing of his idol Kennedy. He had entered the jail car park illegally, but had not been stopped as he walked up and shot Oswald.

Ruby was convicted of murder. He appealed and while awaiting a retrial, was found to have cancer. On 3 January 1967 he died. These bizarre events prompted speculation that Oswald was only a pawn in a conspiracy to eliminate the president, and that he had to be silenced. Ruby was a man of mystery and his part, it was suggested, was not as clear as it seemed.

Oswald, in the short time he lived after the shooting, protested that he was innocent of Kennedy's and the policeman's killing, although there is little doubt he fired the shots that killed Kennedy, and there were witnesses to his shooting of officer Tippit. But were others involved? Such was the speculation and conflicting evidence published that a commission was set up under Earl Warren, chief justice of the US Supreme Court, to investigate. Its conclusions were that Oswald and Ruby

Kennedy's coffin leaves the cathedral after the requiem mass. His widow, Jacqueline, their two children, and Kennedy's brothers follow behind.

had each acted on their own. But, in December 1978, after dozens of books had challenged the Warren Commission's report, the House Select Committee on Assassinations reversed these findings, stating that 'Kennedy was probably assassinated as the result of a conspiracy.' It concluded that probably *two* gunmen fired at him from different points, but was unable to identify any conspirators. Likely candidates, such as Soviet or Cuban agencies, all the US intelligence agencies and organized crime, were 'exonerated'.

The mystery about what really happened continues to fascinate, fed by statistics such as the fact that in the three years after the assassination, 18 key witnesses to the events surrounding Kennedy, Oswald and Ruby had died – only five by 'natural' causes. No fewer than six were shot, two died equally violently (a slashed throat and a karate chop), three died in car accidents and two committed suicide. Only time (and a further reduction in the number of witnesses) seems likely to diminish the flow of words about the case.

A DREAM SHATTERED BY CONSPIRACY?

'I've seen the Promised Land,' he said. 'I may not get there with you . . .' Next day he was shot.

James Earl Ray is escorted to prison to begin his 99-year sentence.

Martin Luther King was assassinated on 4 April 1968. For most of the time since, James Earl Ray has been imprisoned for the crime but, as with the murders of other prominent political figures, there has never been complete agreement that the right man has been held, and there are many who think he was framed.

King was born in Atlanta, Georgia, on 15 January 1929. His father was pastor of the local church and young Martin had a very religious upbringing. The segregation of black children like himself from white children was soon troubling his young intelligence, and he came to appreciate his father's efforts in fighting this policy, and the humiliations he suffered while making no progress. As the boy grew, he himself suffered the same humiliations, and in 1947 he became his father's assistant pastor in order to join the fight.

King continued his education at Boston University, married a fellow student in 1953 and then, in 1954, returned south to Montgomery, Alabama, where he became pastor of Dexter Avenue Baptist Church. He was awarded his Ph.D and was elected to the committee of the National Association for the Advancement of Colored People.

In 1954 the Supreme Court declared segregated schooling unlawful, and in retaliation a campaign of terror, led by the notorious Ku Klux Klan, was waged by white people against blacks in the southern states. In Montgomery King led black people in a boycott of the buses in protest against laws that forbade them to sit next to whites and compelled them to surrender their seats to white people on demand. The bus boycott became an international news item, and ended only when the Supreme Court declared Alabama's bus laws unconstitutional. King's campaign made him a national figure.

Over the next few years King met Vice-President Nixon and President Eisenhower in his attempts to improve the lot of black people. However, his increasing fame did not prevent him, in 1958, from

Martin Luther King with his wife in a Chicago apartment.

being arrested and beaten and, later that year, he was stabbed and badly wounded in New York while signing copies of his book. King preached non-violence, but was imprisoned again in 1960 despite now having the support of the future President Kennedy.

King was jailed again in 1963 during a campaign of police brutality in Birmingham, Alabama. In August that year, a quarter of a million people marched on Washington to demand civil rights for black people, and King made the famous speech, often repeated on video or radio since, in which he described his 'dream'. Soon afterwards President Kennedy was assassinated and King felt that a similar fate might befall him.

In 1964 a Civil Rights Act was passed in the United States, and King was awarded the Nobel Peace Prize. Despite this progress, however, black discontent increased as discrimination continued, and King also became active in an anti-Vietnam War campaign – a war in which blacks were dying while fighting for freedoms they did not possess.

In 1968 King planned a civil disobedience campaign in an attempt to influence government policies. On 3 April he made a speech in Memphis, Tennessee, supporting a strike by sanitation workers. He remarked on threats to his life and commented that they didn't matter to him now. 'I've seen the Promised Land,' he said. 'I may not get there with you, but we as a people *will* get to the Promised Land.'

At 6.01 pm the next day King was standing on the balcony of his room at the Lorraine Motel in Memphis talking to his chauffeur below when he was shot by a single bullet fired, it is alleged, from a bathroom window of a lodging house nearby. The 30.06-calibre bullet from a Remington Gamemaster rifle struck him on the right side of the jaw, passed through his neck and severed his spinal cord. He was rushed to St Joseph's Hospital but there was no chance of saving him and he died an hour later.

The rifle was found wrapped up with other items on the pavement outside the door of the lodging house, as if dropped by the assassin. Fingerprints on it were identified as belonging to James Earl Ray, an escaped convict, and a warrant was issued for his arrest. In May Ray fled to London on a false Canadian passport, and then on to Lisbon, where he hid, but in June he returned to London en route for Brussels and was arrested there. He was sent back to the United States and stood trial for King's murder in March 1969. He pleaded guilty and was sentenced to 99 years' imprisonment, but next day tried to alter his plea to not guilty, insisting on having a new lawyer. Ever since he has protested his innocence, claiming that he was duped into being present in the lodging house that day, but that he had left before the shooting.

Ray, born on 10 March 1928, had dropped out of school and held menial jobs before, at 17, he enlisted in the army. He was discharged after a while for his ineptness and inability to adapt to service life. He drifted into smuggling, burglary, forgery and armed robbery, and in 1960 was sentenced to 20 years in jail for offences committed while on parole. In 1967 he escaped from the Missouri state penitentiary but he was a minor crook and only $50 was offered as a reward for his recapture.

Ray claims that at the time of King's death he was smuggling guns for a man whom he knew as 'Raoul', and that the assassination gun was a sample which he had taken to Memphis on instructions to show to a client. He had left his Memphis room a short while before 6 pm on 4 April and had heard of the assassination of King on his car radio. He had not returned to the room, but had fled to Canada, and subsequently to Europe with the money and passport supplied to him.

Ray's version of events would certainly explain the bundle of incriminating items left outside the lodging house door. Even an unintelligent petty criminal would hardly leave such an obvious trail behind, and it has more the look of a 'plant'.

What has worried many observers since the assassination is the gradually revealed evidence of the FBI's efforts to blacken King's name. The hatred which J. Edgar Hoover, the head of the FBI, felt towards him was increased when King won a Nobel Prize. Hoover ordered the use of many

Ray takes the oath before the House Select Committee on Assassinations in August 1978.

Mrs King (centre) at her husband's funeral.

illegal 'dirty tricks' against him. King's home and office were bugged, his phones were tapped and sexual misdemeanours were discovered which were subsequently made known to Mrs King. The FBI even attempted to persuade King by an anonymous letter to commit suicide rather than accept the Nobel Prize. FBI agents have since come forward to describe the agency's antipathy towards King, and even to claim that there was rejoicing when he was killed.

The CIA were also found to be interested in King and to be holding a detailed file on him. In 1978 the House Select Committee on Assassinations heard from a St Louis man, Russell Byers, that in 1966 or 1967 two men had offered him $50,000 to arrange King's death – a fact which the FBI had known about since 1973 but had not revealed to investigators. Byers suspected that he was being lined up as a fall guy in the way that Ray claimed he was set up.

The Committee came to the conclusion that a conspiracy was likely and heavily criticized the FBI, although finding that 'no federal state or local government agency was involved.'

Subsequent investigations in the 1980s by a British television company unearthed a man who admitted assisting Ray before and after the assassination. This was done on instructions from an FBI agent and a man operating from a CIA undercover office in Montreal, from where Ray was supplied with false identities, including that with which he fled to Europe. In the late 1980s the producers of a programme about the case even claimed to be on the track of 'Raoul'.

Ray escaped for three days in 1969 but, without the support he had had after the killing, he did not get very far.

Whether or not the extent of Ray's guilt in the murder of Martin Luther King is ever properly established, the assassination stands out as a crime committed by evil forces against progress and liberalism.

FAMILY LIFE IN THE DESERT

In his twisted mind he was a Messiah, but his hold over his 'family' led to the most savage of crimes.

On 9 August 1969 a man and two women entered the Hollywood home of the beautiful actress Sharon Tate, while another woman waited outside. Sharon Tate, the wife of the film director Roman Polanski, who was in Europe at the time, was eight months pregnant. In her husband's absence she had two friends staying with her, Voytek Frykowski, a writer, and his girlfriend, Abigail Folger. She had also invited round her former lover Jay Sebring, and there was another person in the house, the 18-year-old Steven Earl Parent, who had called to see Frykowski.

All five people in the house were brutally murdered. The woman who waited outside as a lookout, 21-year-old Linda Kasabian, was to become a witness for the prosecution at the murder trial, and she related a terrible story.

First, she said, there were loud screams from within the house. Then Frykowski crawled outside with blood over him. The two stared into each other's eyes before Frykowski toppled over into the bushes. Kasabian went inside to witness a bloodbath. Some victims were already dead or dying. The man among the intruders, Charles 'Tex' Watson, an ex-footballer, was beating one of the victims on the head. One of the girls, Patricia Krenwinkel, was chasing Sharon Tate with a knife, screaming that she was there to do the Devil's work. Sharon Tate, Kasabian said, was killed last. She pleaded for the life of her baby, but was repeatedly stabbed in the womb, as well as everywhere else on her body. Afterwards a towel dipped in her blood was used to write the word 'pig' on the living room door. The extent of the frenzy of the attack can be grasped from Frykowski's wounds. He was shot twice with a .22 rifle which Watson had taken into the house, struck many times on the head with a blunt instrument and stabbed no fewer than 51 times.

The discovery of the murders and the apparently senseless degree of violence involved shocked the whole of America, the feelings of horror being reinforced two nights later when Leno La Bianca, a supermarket owner, and his wife Rosemary were slaughtered in similar manner in their house near to the Polanskis', the word 'war' being scored on his stomach.

The second of the women in the house when Sharon Tate and her friends were killed was Susan Atkins, and it was through her that the gang was finally captured. When she and others were subsequently under arrest for stealing cars, she dropped hints to her cell mate about the murders of Sharon Tate and the La Biancas. Her remarks were passed on to other prisoners and eventually to the police. She was

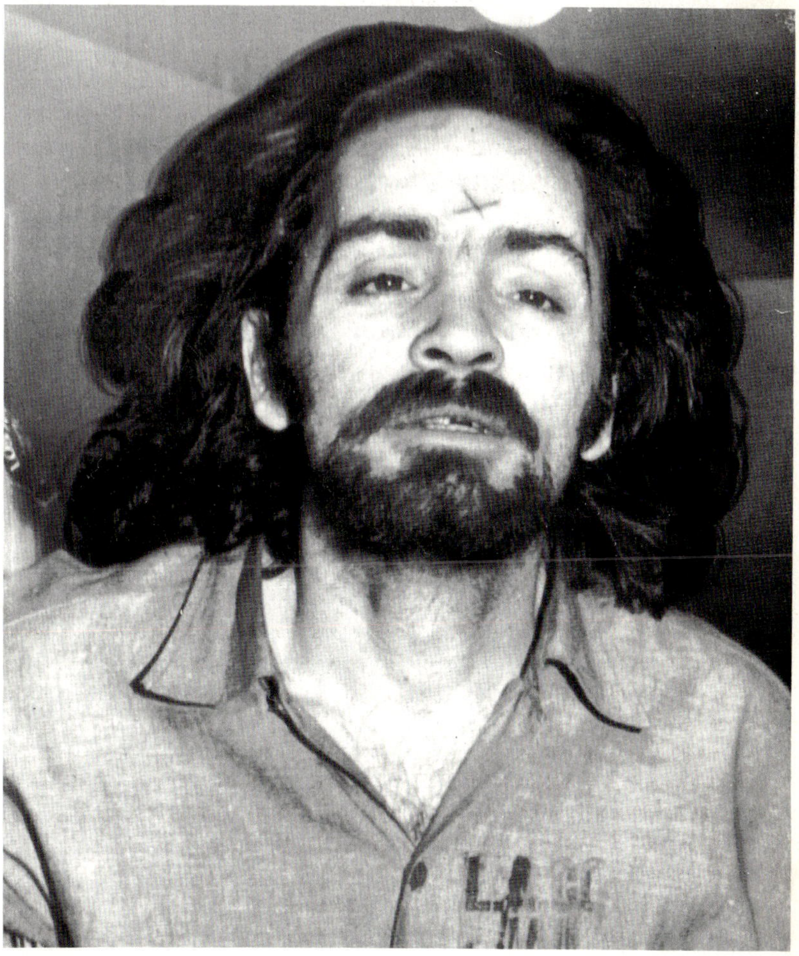

Charles Manson on his way to court.

questioned, and police investigations led to a large 'hippie family' and to its leader, Charles Manson.

Manson was born in Cincinnati, Ohio, on 11 November 1934. His unmarried mother, Kathleen Maddox, was a prostitute, who was jailed when Manson was a boy for beating up and robbing her clients, with the aid of her brother. At the age of 11 Manson, already a juvenile delinquent, was sent to a reform school. Various sentences for theft and pimping meant that he was to spend nearly 23 years in some form of custody or other. When at 32 he at last acquired some freedom, he was bitter and ill-adapted to lead a normal life. He gravitated to the Haight-Ashbury district of San Francisco, at the time the centre of the 'psychedelic flower-power' hippie movement. He grew long hair and a beard, played the guitar, developed a deep interest in hypnotism and the occult, and with his hypnotic eyes soon had a circle of girls at his feet.

Manson, in fact, had such command over women in many levels of society that he began to see himself as some sort of messiah, his name 'Man's son' becoming a kind of confirmation of his singularity. He admired the Beatles and interpreted the lyrics of their song 'Helter Skelter' as an indication that there would be a black uprising against white people.

Before this could happen, Manson decided to lead his followers, called his 'family', into the Californian desert. There they lived as a commune in abandoned shacks at the rear of a ranch. The population shifted, but Manson was always the 'god'. He despised women, although they always outnumbered the men. The women were subservient and were forbidden to question his decisions. They had to submit sexually to any man who wanted them, and indeed at the murder trial Linda Kasabian, under cross-examination, was forced to admit that she did not know who the father of her second child was. Manson banned contraceptives as he did alcohol. Drugs and sex were very much the order of the day.

Manson exerted such influence over his followers that he was able to command them to commit crimes, beginning with petty theft and car stealing. Terrorizing rich people in their homes came next, and this in turn led to the murders. Manson had not been present but had instigated the orgy of violence. It was his hatred of the rich and privileged that prompted the choice of victims. It is believed that he had been a guest of the Polanskis before the murder, and had a 'hit list' of wealthy and famous names in the film colony. The daubing of the word 'pig', and then of 'rise' and 'healter skelter' (*sic*), which appeared

Right
Police standing guard outside Sharon Tate's home following the discovery of five bodies.

in blood on the wall at the La Biancas, was meant to suggest that the 'black uprising' was under way, and was intended to assist its progress.

Manson went on trial for the murders alongside the 22-year-olds, Susan Atkins and Patricia Krenwinkel, and another female follower, the 20-year-old Leslie Van Houten, who was charged only with the La Bianca murders. Charles Watson was to be tried separately, being held in Texas when the main trial started.

Left
Sharon Tate after her marriage to Roman Polanski.

Top right
Linda Kasabian, who acted as lookout for the murderers.
Above right
Susan Atkins, one of the accused in the murder trial.
Below right
Patricia Krenwinkel, another of the accused.
Bottom right
Leslie van Houten, who was charged with the murders of the La Bianca couple.

There were 84 witnesses in the trial, which lasted nine months. During this time the horrors of Manson and his way of life, his distorted views and his hypnotic hold over his followers were fully aired.

Manson's power over his females was apparent when he hatched a plan for the three on trial with him to take the stand and confess, at the same time exonerating him. This, however, did not happen because, first of all, the lawyers for the girls refused to co-operate and question them, and secondly because the judge ruled that if they wanted to tell their stories as narrative, they would have to do so without the jury being present. Their testimony would be edited for the jury, who would not hear the inadmissible parts. The girls then refused to give evidence at all, which meant that their defence rested.

Manson, however, now decided to take the stand, and he, in the absence of the jury and in a quiet and sometimes tearful manner, expounded some of his philosophy. Wearing a cross cut on his forehead, the sign of an outcast, which the three girls had copied, he ran through the story of his life. The members of his 'family', he claimed, were rejected people – 'people alongside the road', whom he took and taught that love could not be wrong. He was bitter about the lack of love in a society which had cast him as a fiend and deprived him of any worthwhile life for so many years. His peace, he said, was in the desert sunshine or in his prison cell, which he preferred to life in normal society. When he had had his say, he told the girls not to testify.

All four defendants were found guilty, Manson being described as 'one of the most evil, satanic men who ever walked the face of the earth'. He was convicted of nine murders, his other victims being Donald 'Shorty' Shea, a bit-part player and stuntman, and Gary Hinman, a musician.

All the defendants were sentenced to death in the gas chamber but, capital punishment having been abolished in California, they began to serve prison sentences. Manson, with nine life sentences and apparently unrepentant, became caretaker of the chapel in the prison at Vacaville in southern California.

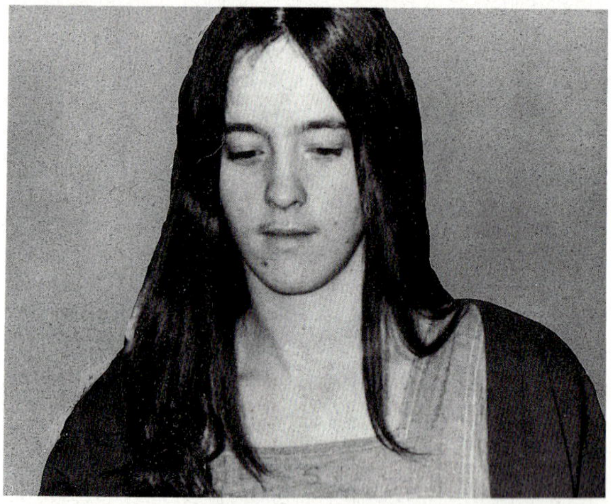

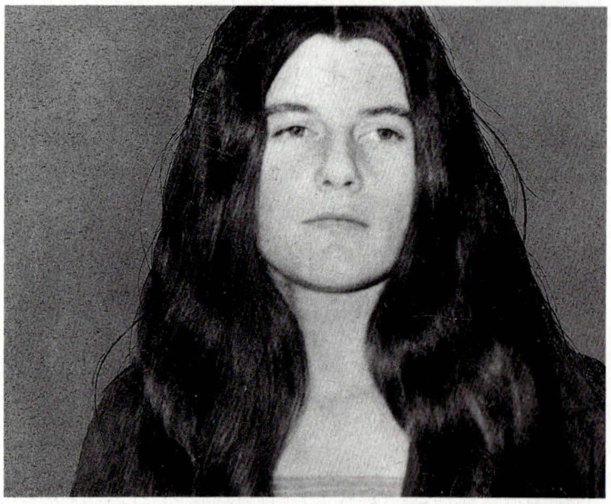

Opposite
Digging for the remains of Donald Shea, one of Manson's victims.

Merrill Lynch

The Last Two Decades

A missing missionary,
a killer clown,
a Son of Sam,
a murdered musician,
a latter-day Ripper and
a disappearing dingo.

The police van carrying Peter Sutcliffe enters the Old Bailey, London.

MISS McKINNEY AND THE MISSING MORMON MISSIONARY

The 'sex-in-chains' case was a story that had everything except an ending – but the middle bit had everybody entertained.

Joyce McKinney being taken, rather unwillingly, to court.

The holder of the title 'Miss North Carolina High School' could naturally be expected to grow into a beautiful woman and Joyce McKinney did so. She was also pious and romantic and, when she met a handsome young Mormon missionary, it was love at first sight. She determined that he would be her man and pursued him with the ardour of any heroine in the romantic novels of, say, Barbara Cartland.

How then, can her story be included in a volume dealing with crime – especially when nobody was convicted of anything and nobody came to any real harm? The answer is that what happened in England in 1977, while hardly a 'crime', was certainly a case and one which filled the newspapers and kept the public entertained for weeks with its salacious details.

It all began like a pulp-fiction romance in

1975. Miss McKinney was showing a friend how her new motor car – a Stingray convertible – handled. They had been for a drive and were sitting chatting when a man leaned in at the window to ask a question. Miss McKinney found herself suddenly looking deep into the bluest pair of eyes she had ever seen. Readers of romantic fiction will know what followed. 'My heart did flip-flops', said Miss McKinney, not being the mistress of the genre that Miss Cartland is.

The eyes belonged to 6ft-2in, 19-year-old Kirk Anderson, a young man preparing to be a Mormon missionary at Salt Lake City. He was eight years younger than Miss McKinney, but Miss McKinney was terribly in love and was soon having a passionate affair with him. 'Every time he kissed me it was bombs, firecrackers, the Fourth of July', she said.

However, as readers of romance know, there is no story if the course of true love always runs smooth and to Miss McKinney's desolation, Anderson broke off the relationship. And now she ceased to behave in the manner approved of in romantic fiction: she began to harass Anderson. According to him, windows at his home were smashed. His car was damaged – even rammed. He moved to California, but she followed, and so in desperation he volunteered to continue doing his good work in England.

Miss McKinney formulated a crazy plan to capture Anderson, and placed an advertisement in a paper for 'a muscle man, a pilot and a preacher'. The story might have now taken on the character of a television adventure – *The A Team* combined with *Mission Impossible* – but she failed to collect her helpers.

Miss McKinney nevertheless made her way to England and continued her pursuit of Anderson – from East Grinstead, through Reading to Milton Gardens, Epsom. None of these places has ever been a venue of romantic fiction, so the story transforms itself into a mystery – Kirk Anderson disappeared for three days.

When he resurfaced, on 17 September 1977, the story assumed the aspect that finally took it to the front pages of the

Kirk Anderson, the object of Joyce McKinney's affections, leaving court.

newspapers. He claimed he had been kidnapped, and held, handcuffed and manacled, on the orders, so it was reported, of a 'wealthy, lovesick woman'.

The police investigated, and Miss McKinney, together with an accomplice, Keith May, was charged with abducting Anderson. At the preliminary hearing, in November, Anderson's story was told. He claimed that Miss McKinney and May had approached him outside his church and, by threatening him with what turned out to be an imitation .38 revolver, had persuaded him into a car, where chloroform was used to keep him quiet during a drive to a cottage previously hired by Miss McKinney in Devon. He was held there forcibly, while McKinney informed him that marriage with her would be the price of his freedom.

Anderson said that May tied him to a

Far right
Models wearing the Mormon one-piece undergarment designed to 'lock out lust'.

bed with chains and a leather strap. Miss McKinney then aroused him with oral sex and, claiming that his ransom would be a baby, had her way with him in what was described in court as 'female rape'.

A couple of nights later, Anderson claimed, she entered the room again in her negligee, put on some records and was clearly intent in repeating the experience of before but with a more complaisant lover. He demurred, settling instead for a back rub. Miss McKinney, however, merely fetched May who, with chains, ropes and padlocks, tied Anderson's arms and legs to the four bedposts, leaving him spreadeagled on his back.

Miss McKinney now tore the pyjamas from him – and also an undergarment which caused great speculation in the court. It was described as a kind of Mormon male chastity belt. This sacred item, Anderson said, he had since burnt, this being the correct way to dispose of a desecrated religious object. Naturally, Miss McKinney again satisfied her lusts on his helpless body.

Miss McKinney, of course, told a very different version of the events. She was to claim later that she had studied pornographic movies in order to learn techniques designed to overcome Anderson's sexual inhibitions. She had been obliged to do outrageous things to him in bed. Bondage games became part of their relationship and, according to Miss McKinney, everything that happened in Devon was consented to and thoroughly enjoyed by Anderson. She loved him so much, she said, that for him she would have 'skied down Mount Everest in the nude with a carnation up her nose'.

Right
McKinney and May on their way to report to the police station.

May and McKinney were committed for trial, being in the meantime granted bail. The press looked forward to the trial proper for more sensational revelations in what they had called the 'sex-in-chains' case. But the papers and their readers were to be disappointed. Miss McKinney, who had entered Britain on a false passport, managed to leave the country posing as a deaf-mute. She arrived in Canada dressed as a nun.

The British authorities showed no urgency in their efforts to extradite her, and the British press was obliged to satisfy its readers by paying for confessions and obtaining a photograph of Miss McKinney in the nude. Slowly the story died down, with Joyce McKinney's admission that the Mormon church had overcome the power of her love in the battle for Anderson.

However, as readers of Barbara Cartland know, in romantic fiction love is not easily conquered and there is always a new twist to the story on the next page. In 1984 Miss McKinney, now 35, was arrested and charged with disturbing the peace outside Kirk Anderson's office back in Salt Lake City. Maybe there is still a surprise to come in the final chapter.

THE CLOWN WHO WAS A KILLER

Pogo the Clown was popular with children at Democrat fund-raising parties, but his garden held a terrible secret.

One of John Wayne Gacy's proudest possessions was a photograph of himself with Rosalynn Carter, the 'First Lady' of the United States, which she had kindly signed for him. It was in recognition of his good work for the children of the suburb of Chicago in which he lived and for his contributions to the Democratic Party and President Jimmy Carter's re-election fund.

Gacy had earned the respect of his neighbourhood, which he had not always commanded. A fat man, he had at first found it difficult to get people to take him seriously. But he had cashed in on his oddness by becoming 'Pogo the Clown', a highly successful entertainer at children's parties and local functions, particularly those with a political motive. He was also very successful in business, building up a profitable construction firm, the PDM

John Gacy with Rosalynn Carter at a reception in Chicago.

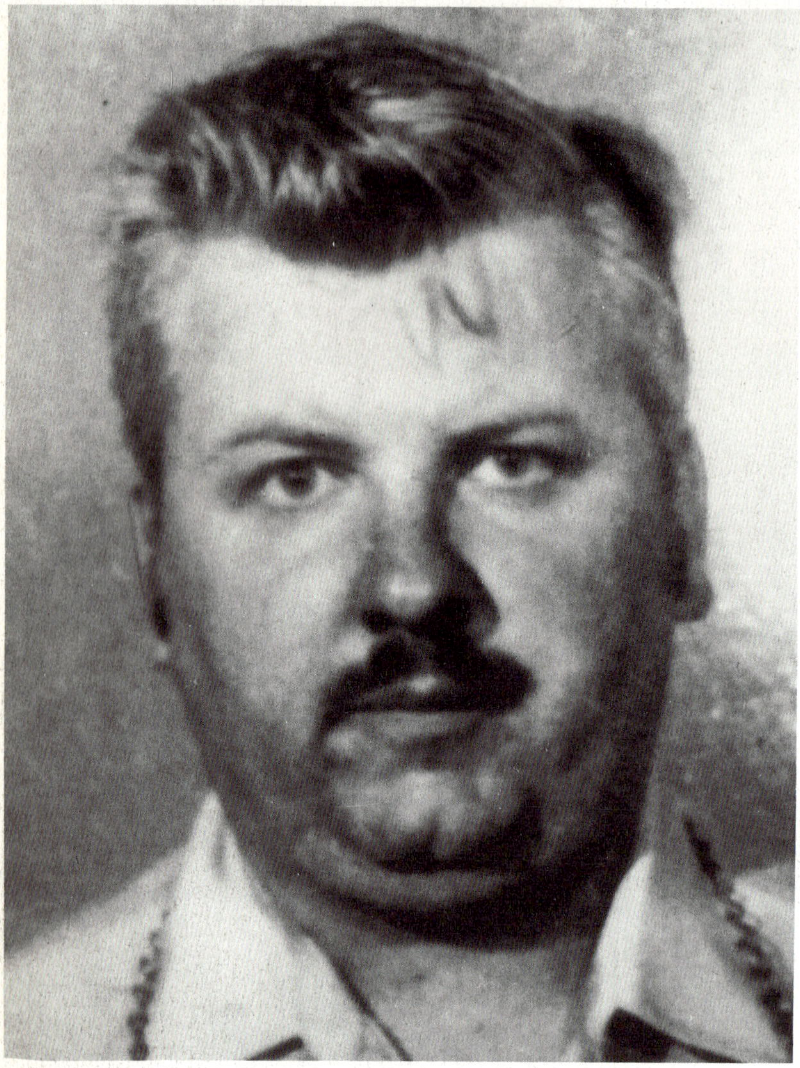

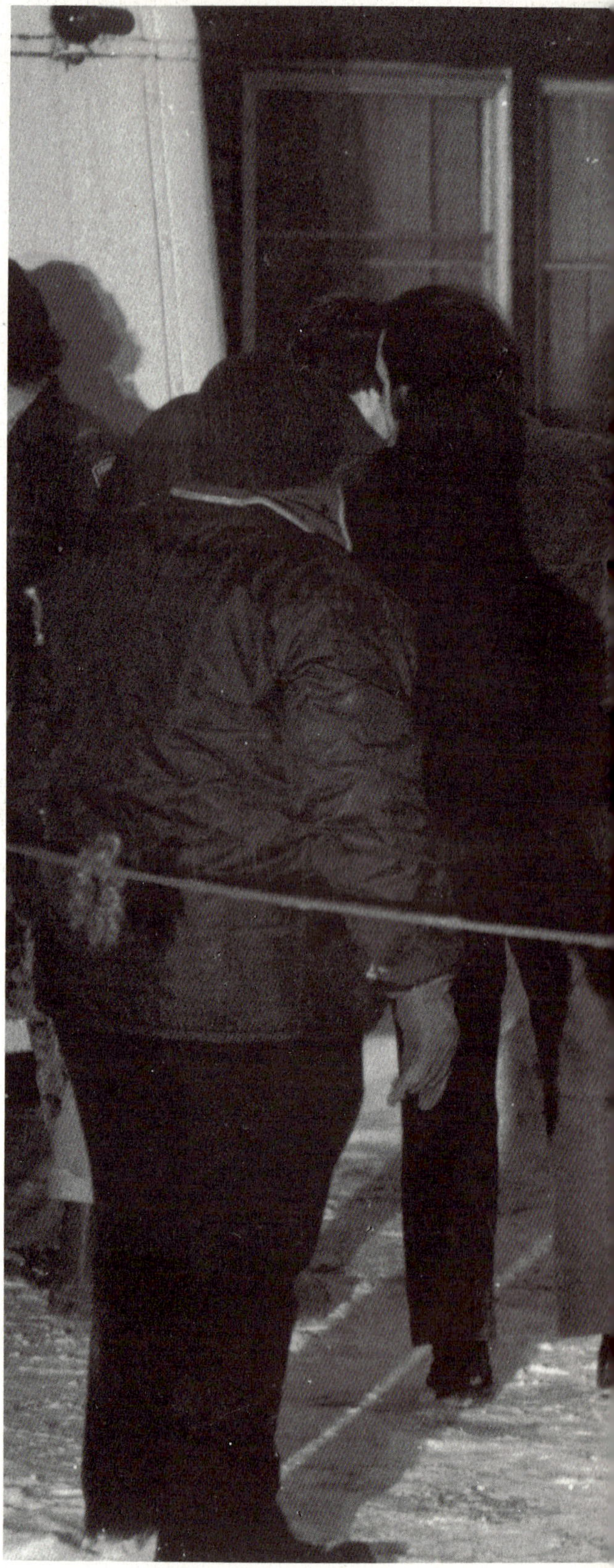

Above
Gacy was eventually convicted of murdering 33 boys and youths.

Contracting Company. He was less successful in marriage. He had married in 1967, but after two years and two children his wife divorced him. He married again, three years later, but this union lasted only four years. Both wives were to claim that he beat them.

Gacy was not all he seemed, however, as events near the end of 1978 showed. On 11 December Robert Piest, a 15-year-old boy, disappeared from a pharmacy in Des Plaines, Illinois, having asked his mother to wait for him, as he was going to talk to a building contractor about a job. Enquiries by the police led them to the 38-year-old Gacy, who admitted he had spoken to Piest, but did not know anything of his whereabouts. But Piest was not the first local youth to disappear – in fact for six years police had been worried about a whole epidemic of missing youths. Several times previously in their enquiries Gacy had appeared on the files, sometimes as a possible suspect. Moreover, he had two convictions for sexual assaults on young men.

With public disquiet about the affair growing, police questioned Gacy with more vigour than before, and instituted a search of his luxury ranch at Summerdale, Illinois. Soon, digging in the garden began

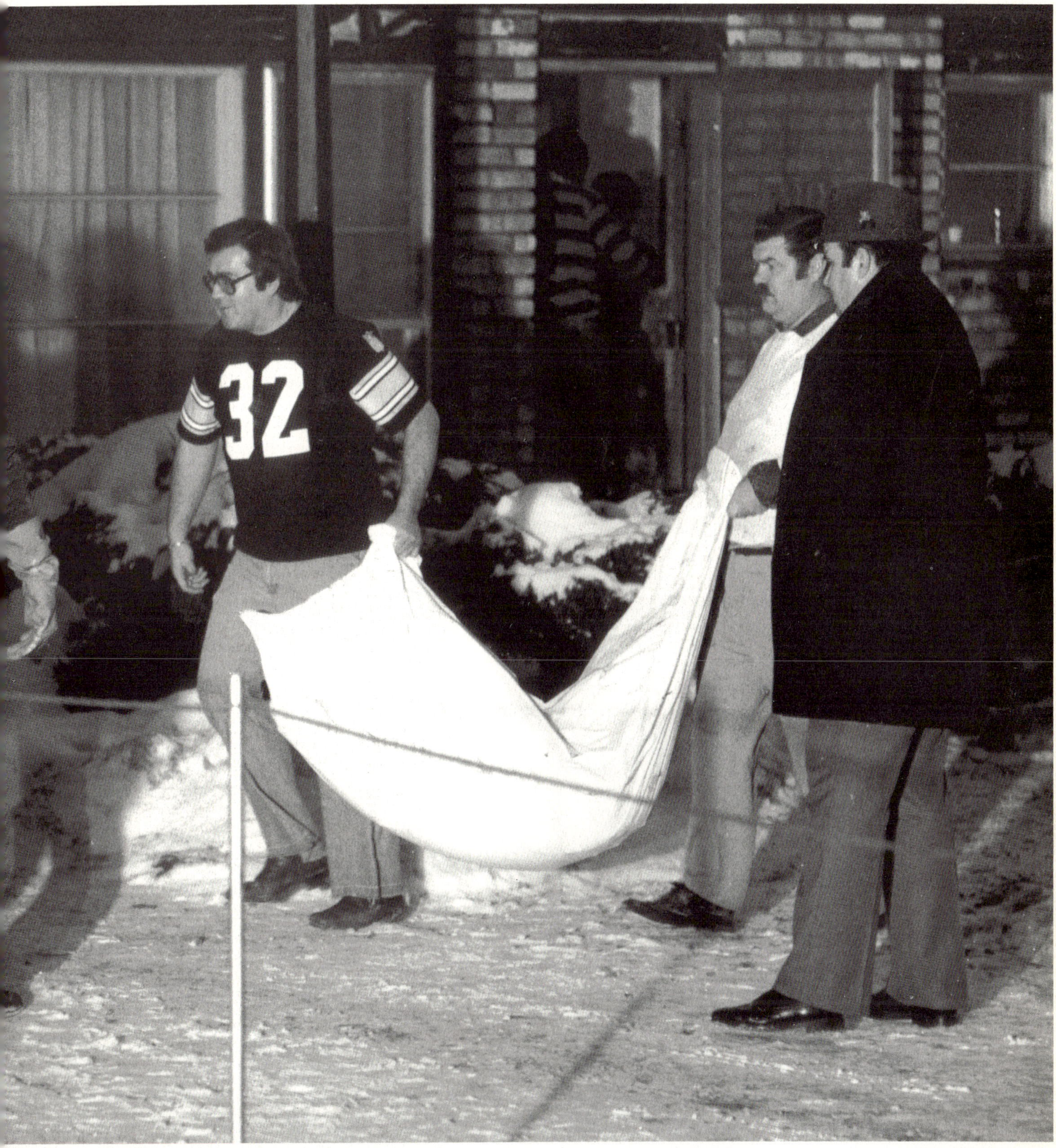

to reveal bodies. Knowing that he could protest his innocence no longer, Gacy then drew the police a map of the space around his home and, with the directions he supplied, the bodies of 28 boys and youths were discovered. Gacy also admitted murdering five more boys and throwing the bodies in the Des Plaines river. Frogmen were able to find them.

Gacy's history began to be filled in. Dominated by his mother and sister as a youngster, he had never been at ease with women, and had always preferred boys as his partners. The work force of his company had been recruited from the large band of young, out-of-work local youths or

Police bringing out a body from Gacy's house – 28 victims were found buried beneath the foundations and on various parts of his property.

Above
Some of the unfortunate young men whom Gacy first sexually abused and then strangled.
Below
David Cram who lived with Gacy and helped to dig holes which were later used as graves.

from those flocking into Chicago and arriving at the Greyhound bus station. He treated his employees well – except, of course, for those who ended up in his garden.

His second wife related how, towards the end of their marriage, he began staying out at night and showing an interest in

pornographic photographs of men. It transpired that his nights were spent in a part of Chicago known as Bughouse Square, an area frequented by homosexuals.

Gacy would take his victims home and either chloroform them or trick them into being handcuffed. They would then be the victims of acts of sodomy, being afterwards killed by strangulation.

At the time of Gacy's trial in 1979 Illinois was considering reintroducing the death penalty for certain classes of murder and the prosecutor asked for execution by lethal injection. Gacy's only defence was insanity, but his murders were so carefully planned that the plea failed and he was convicted and sentenced to life imprisonment.

The neighbours of the wealthy, respected Gacy were shocked when he was arrested. When his story became known and it was realized how often he had slipped through the police net during six years of wholesale murder, the local citizens berated the police for their incompetence.

It is ironic that John Wayne Gacy had been named after one of America's most famous heroes of the entertainment world. He, too, was to become as famous for a while, but his nickname was not nearly so respectful as that of 'the Duke'. Gacy was known as 'the Killer Clown'.

THE DREADED SON OF SAM

A parking ticket and a woman walking her dog caught New York's infamous killer.

A killer who appeared to choose his victims at random left New Yorkers terror-stricken for several months in 1977. Police were quite powerless to stop him, but an alert lady walking her dog was eventually to prove the means of his capture. In addition she probably saved several lives.

The killer began attacking women on Christmas Eve 1975, wielding a knife. However in July 1976, now using a .44 calibre gun, he committed his first murder. Two girls were sitting talking in an Oldsmobile in Buhre Avenue, New York, at 1 am in the morning when a man approached, took a gun from a paper bag and fired five shots at them through the windscreen. One girl, Donna Lauria, was killed, and her friend injured.

On 23 October a couple were sitting in a sports car in Flushing, New York, when several shots were fired at them. The man was injured and a .44 bullet was found in the car. On 26 November two girls were chatting on the verandah in front of a house in Queens, New York, when, at about 12.30 am, a man approached and began asking the way but, before finishing his question, he produced a gun and shot at the girls. Both were wounded, one very badly. Bullets found showed that the same .44 gun had been used as in the murder of Donna Lauria.

A second death was marked against the killer on 30 January 1977 when a courting couple in a car in Ridgewood, New York, were fired upon. The woman, Christine Freund, died.

Most of the killer's victims had been in pairs in parked cars, but this pattern was broken on 8 March 1977, when a girl walking alone, Virginia Voskerichian, was shot in the face by the killer and died at once. This was less than a quarter of a mile from where Christine Freund had been shot, and made local people extremely nervous. The police by now had recognized that the bullets in all these cases came from

David Berkowitz on his way to court under police escort.

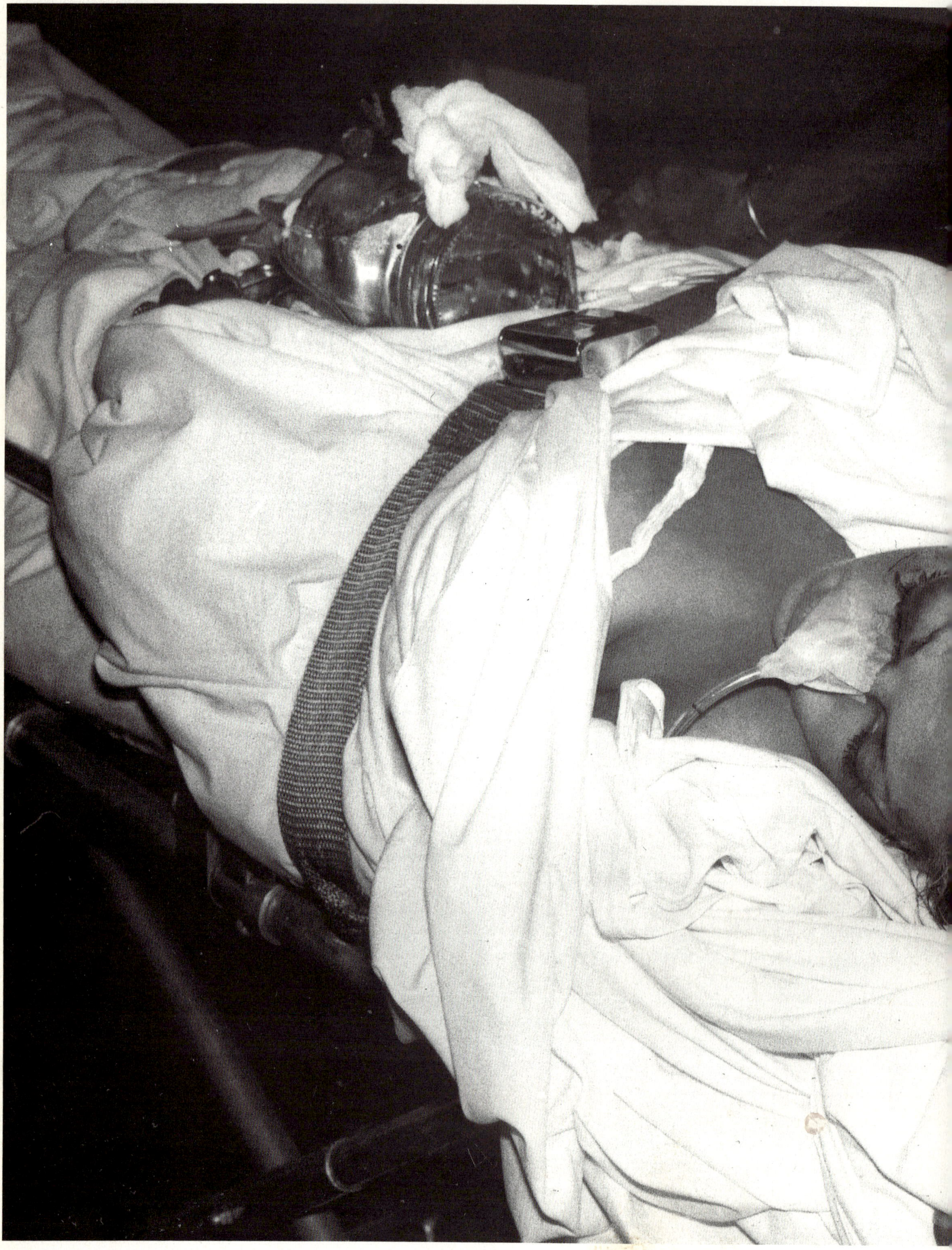

Left
Stacy Moskowitz being rushed to the operating theatre in an unavailing effort to save her life.

the same .44 gun, and warned the public of a psychopath who could strike at any time against anybody. There was no lead to his identity – even descriptions from those who had seen him failed to correspond. Mayor Beame of New York called a press conference to alert the public and ordered the police to make every effort to catch the killer. A special squad was formed, and plain-clothes patrols watched the area in which he had selected his victims.

It was not long before there were more deaths. On 17 April Alexander Esau and Valentina Suriani were sitting in their car in the Bronx, not far from the scene of the first murder, when both were shot dead through the windscreen. This time the killer left a letter in the road to Captain Joseph Borrelli of the police. 'I am deeply hurt by your calling me a weman-hater (*sic*),' it said. 'I am not. But I am a monster. I am the Son of Sam. . . . I love prowling the streets looking for fair game. . . . The wemen of Queens are prettyest (*sic*) of all. . . .'

'Son of Sam' was by now compelling New Yorkers to change their habits. They tried not to be sitting in their parked cars after midnight, particularly in the Queens and Bronx areas. On 26 June 1977 a young couple were saying goodnight in a car parked outside a house in Queens when the killer fired four shots at them through the windscreen. Both were hit, but recovered.

A month later, on 29 July, all police resources were on the lookout in Queens and the Bronx. The murderer's strikes seemed to occur at intervals of a few weeks, and this was the anniversary of the first killing. But the night passed without incident.

Two nights later, however, at 1.30 am in another area of New York, on the Brooklyn shore facing Coney Island, the killer fired four shots through the windscreen of a car at a courting couple. The girl, Stacy Moskowitz, was fatally wounded; her boyfriend, Robert Violante, was blinded.

This proved to be Son of Sam's last strike, and it is where the woman taking her dog for a walk enters the picture. She had noticed two policemen placing a ticket

Valentina Suriani and Alexander Esau, two of the victims of Son of Sam.

on a car parked near a fire hydrant on nearby Bay 16th Street around the time of the murder. Then she saw a man run up to the car and drive off as soon as the police had gone. She reported the incident and, because only one ticket had been issued for parking by a hydrant that night, the police were able quickly to check on the owner. He was David Berkowitz, aged 24, of 25 Pine Street, Yonkers.

Three days later the police found his Ford Galaxy in front of his apartment building and kept watch on it. When Berkowitz came to use it, Detective Inspector Tim Dowd challenged him and Berkowitz readily admitted that he was the Son of Sam.

The killer who had kept New Yorkers in a state of anxiety for months turned out to be a slightly podgy man with a soft smile and pleasant eyes. Police thought at first he was mentally retarded, and he was certainly not particularly bright. Friends were to say he was a lonely man who ate junk food, with a particular liking for chocolate ice-cream. He lived in a room from which he did not clear the rubbish and in which he wrote messages on the walls. An illegitimate child (although brought up by Nat Berkowitz, his 'father'), he apparently always felt unwanted, and had developed an obsession about his unattractiveness to women.

Berkowitz did not know who his real

Christine Freund (left) was fatally wounded but Judy Placido survived.

father was and probably called himself 'Son of Sam' after a neighbour in Pine Street, Sam Carr, although he was not friendly with Carr. During the period of his murderous assaults he shot and injured Carr's dog which, he was to claim at his trial, had bewitched him.

Berkowitz pleaded guilty and was sentenced to 365 years' imprisonment. He spends the time in writing letters to politicians and newspapers, and claims that he was a member of a satanic cult which performed the killings – one of the messages on the wall of his room in Pine Street was 'Kill for my Master'. Some observers incline to the view that he did not operate alone, noting that descriptions of the killer varied and that the letters from Son of Sam (there were several to newspapers and police) were not all in Berkowitz's handwriting. Moreover, the fact that Sam Carr's sons died in suspicious circumstances after Berkowitz was jailed has been suggested by some as lending support to this theory.

Berkowitz, shy of women when at liberty, now sends suggestive letters to those who write to him. He is one of those lonely killers who murder in order to make themselves important, and he has, in fact, succeeded in a way by transforming himself from an abject nobody into a somebody. He has even earned substantial sums from articles and the sale of film rights in his life story, and his apartment block has become one of the sights of New York.

THE SHOOTING OF A STAR

He saw himself as the Catcher in the Rye, and as John Lennon, in a* Double Fantasy *that led to murder.

John Lennon was a member of the most famous pop group of all – the Beatles. Indeed, at one stage of the group's fame Lennon had angered many Americans by remarking that 'we are more popular than Jesus, now', a statement for which he prudently apologized after thousands of affronted fans had publicly smashed Beatles records and made bonfires of albums.

Lennon was always outspoken and always something of a law unto himself. Born on 9 October 1940, he had studied art, and in his spare time formed a rock band. At the age of 15 he met Paul McCartney, who was 20 months his junior, and the two formed a partnership which composed dozens of hit songs, and was also the nucleus of what became the Beatles. Lennon, being the older, was always regarded in the early days as being the leader of the group, as some of its early names indicate: Johnny and the Moondogs, Long John and the Silver Beatles.

Eventually the group became the Beatles, and earned a cult popularity at the Cavern, the damp cellar of an old warehouse near the Liverpool docks which became famous around the world. The Beatles' first appearance was on 21 March 1961 and over the next two years they performed there nearly 300 times. During this period they made records which topped the charts on both sides of the Atlantic. They also appeared on *The Ed Sullivan Show* in New York, watched by an estimated 73 million television viewers. It has, in fact, been claimed that, while the

John Lennon and Yoko Ono in New York.

Mark David Chapman in 1975 when he was working in a resettlement camp for Vietnamese refugees.

programme was running, not a single crime was committed by a teenager in the whole of the United States.

In the next few years the Beatles led remarkable lives, finding that public appearances frequently became an ordeal as emotional fans tore at their clothing for souvenirs. They changed fashions in dress and hairstyles all over the world, while their rewards from films and records ran into several millions a year in pounds, dollars and other currencies.

In 1970 the group broke up. Two years earlier Lennon had been divorced by his first wife and in 1969 he married Yoko Ono, the daughter of a wealthy Tokyo banker and seven years his senior. She was an artist, and the two had made a notorious record together, appearing naked on the sleeve.

In 1971 the couple left England to live in the United States. They experimented with forms of self-analysis and drugs, and in 1972 were served with a deportation order arising from a drug conviction Lennon had received in London – an order reversed on a 2–1 vote by the New York Supreme Court in 1975. In 1980 Lennon began composing again, and in November released an album called *Double Fantasy.*

It was this new album that Lennon was asked to autograph as he and Yoko Ono left their apartment building, the celebrated Dakota block in New York City, soon after 4.30 pm on 8 December 1980. The man who requested his signature was 25-year-old Mark David Chapman, who had been waiting in the cold most of the day. Lennon signed 'John Lennon, 1980'.

Chapman was apparently pleased with his autograph but, after Lennon had left for a recording session, he continued to wait, telling the doorman that he wanted to get Yoko Ono's signature as well. With two pairs of long pants on, as well as jacket, overcoat and hat, he was well prepared to withstand the cold. At 11 pm Lennon and his wife returned by car and began to cross the sidewalk to the courtyard of the Dakota building. As they did so Chapman stepped out of the shadows and called 'Mr Lennon'. Lennon turned, and Chapman assumed a military firing posture, crouching with legs apart. He raised a .38 Charter Arms revolver and fired five shots, hitting Lennon in chest, back and arm. Lennon staggered and collapsed, while Chapman tossed aside the gun and sat down by the Dakota building. From his jacket pocket he took a well-used copy of J. D. Salinger's novel *The Catcher in the Rye* and began reading it. Lennon was rushed to the Roosevelt Hospital by a patrolman whose job was to shepherd fans around the Dakota, but by the time he reached the emergency room he had died from his wounds. Chapman was arrested without resistance and was found to have 14 Beatles tapes and $2000 in his pockets.

Mark Chapman was born on 10 May 1955 at Fort Worth, Texas, but was brought up in Atlanta and Decatur,

Georgia. At high school he started a rock band based on the Beatles and played guitar like Lennon. After graduating he worked for charitable organizations like the YMCA and continued to acquire Beatles records until his collection was complete. He experimented with drugs, but rejected them and became a born-again Christian. Lennon's remark about Jesus caused him great distress, since Chapman seemed to be acting out a fantasy in which he *was* John Lennon.

In 1977 Chapman went to live in Hawaii and his fantasizing increased. In 1979 he married Gloria H. Abe, a travel agent who was four years his senior and of Japanese descent, thus emulating Lennon to a degree. He got a job as a security guard in a Honolulu apartment building.

Chapman's personality began to deteriorate. He tried to isolate his wife from newspapers, television and even former friends. He spent most of his own spare time playing Beatles records, eating peanuts or visiting art galleries.

In the autumn of 1980 he left his wife and changed the name-tag on his uniform to 'John Lennon'. On 23 October he resigned his job. He signed his last entry in the checking-out book as 'John Lennon',

Lennon fans in Central Park, New York, grieving over the death of their idol.

but on second thoughts crossed it out.

Chapman by now believed that *he* was John Lennon and that the actual songwriter was a fake. Before 'retiring' (like Lennon) he had sold a Norman Rockwell painting and had bought his revolver. He made enquiries of the Federal Aviation Administration about transporting it by plane and was told that the change in air pressure might damage bullets. Six days after leaving his job he flew to New York, with the gun in his baggage but without bullets. In New York he was unable to buy bullets, so flew back to Honolulu. He made an appointment for 26 November to be seen at the Makiki Mental Health Clinic, but did not keep it, and on 6 December flew back to New York, this time taking both his gun and bullets.

That night Chapman stayed at the West Side YMCA, but next day he checked into the Sheraton Centre Hotel and began his wait for Lennon outside the Dakota building. After his arrest Chapman was taken to a psychiatric prison and, at the preliminary hearing following the charge of murder, it was revealed that in 1977 he had attempted suicide and had received psychiatric treatment in hospital. Now in another mental hospital where he was remanded awaiting trial, he was closely guarded in case he should attempt suicide again. His lawyer meanwhile prepared a defence based on a plea of 'not guilty through insanity'. Psychiatrists were prepared to testify that he was certainly insane.

However, on 22 June 1981, Chapman told a judge that God had instructed him to confess to the murder of John Lennon and, against the wishes of his lawyer, Jonathan Marks, he pleaded guilty. Marks was to ask the judge not to impose a minimum sentence, saying that Chapman was not a sane man and had an incurable disease.

The prosecution's case was simply that the murder was deliberately planned and carried out, and that Chapman showed no remorse for his deed.

Chapman, who was wearing a bulletproof vest in court to foil any attempt to assassinate him, was asked if he had anything to say in his defence. He merely read out a passage from his prized copy of *The Catcher in the Rye*, which had clearly made a deep impression on his unbalanced mind. The book examines the adolescent attitudes of its anti-hero narrator, Holden Caulfield, and Chapman quoted the passage in which Caulfield imagines himself standing on the edge of a cliff, watching thousands of children playing:

'What I have to do, I have to catch everybody if they start to go over the cliff – I mean if they're running and they don't look where they're going I have to come out from somewhere and catch them. That's all I'd do all

A mourner affixes a photograph of John Lennon to the gates of the Dakota building.

day. I'd just be the catcher in the rye.'

The meaning of this passage for Chapman was that children needed to be saved from the phoney world of adulthood.

On 24 August 1981 Chapman was sentenced to 20-years-to-life imprisonment for the murder of John Lennon, which meant he would not be eligible for parole for 20 years. He was taken to Sing Sing prison, and his lawyer reported that he did not intend to speak again. He took his book with him and continues to re-read it.

President-elect Ronald Reagan called the death of John Lennon 'a great tragedy.' Ironically, the 25-year-old John W. Hinckley, Jnr, thought similarly, and later recorded on his tape-machine an end-of-1980 message to the old year, which was: 'Nothing, total misery, total death. John Lennon is dead. The world is over. Forget it.' On 30 March 1981 Hinckley went out and shot President Reagan, firing several bullets at him. The President, hit once, survived, but three of his staff were also wounded, one seriously. Hinckley, charged with attempted murder, was later acquitted on the grounds of insanity and committed to a mental institution. He is the same age as Chapman.

THE YORKSHIRE RIPPER

A fake taped message and police errors prolonged a string of savage killings in northern England.

For over five years, starting in 1975, a series of murders, centred on the city of Leeds in Yorkshire, grabbed the headlines in the British press and alerted the public to the fact that a maniac was on the loose. The victims were women and their bodies were horribly mutilated. Usually their skulls were smashed in with a heavy instrument and they were then stabbed with a knife or a screwdriver – anything up to 50 times.

The killer's early victims were prostitutes, and the manner of his bloody attacks on the bodies led quickly to comparisons with the most infamous murderer of all – 'Jack the Ripper'. Soon the press were calling the unknown murderer 'the Yorkshire Ripper'.

The macabre similarity was reinforced by a sequence of events beginning in 1978. The original Jack the Ripper had written to the Central News Agency: 'I keep on hearing the police have caught me but they won't fix me just yet. . . . I am down on whores and I shan't quit ripping them till I do get buckled.' Subsequent messages taunted the police. During the Yorkshire Ripper's career of terror the police began receiving letters signed 'Jack the Ripper' and then a cassette purporting to be from him. Communications technology had apparently given the new Ripper a more up-to-date and horribly fascinating method of contacting the police, but the crimes and the messages were similar: 'You are no nearer catching me than when I started.'

The police had first warned about a vicious killer who might strike again after the discovery of the severely mutilated

Peter Sutcliffe and his wife, Sonia, on their wedding day.

Right
The first three victims of the Yorkshire Ripper, all prostitutes, were killed in the space of five months.

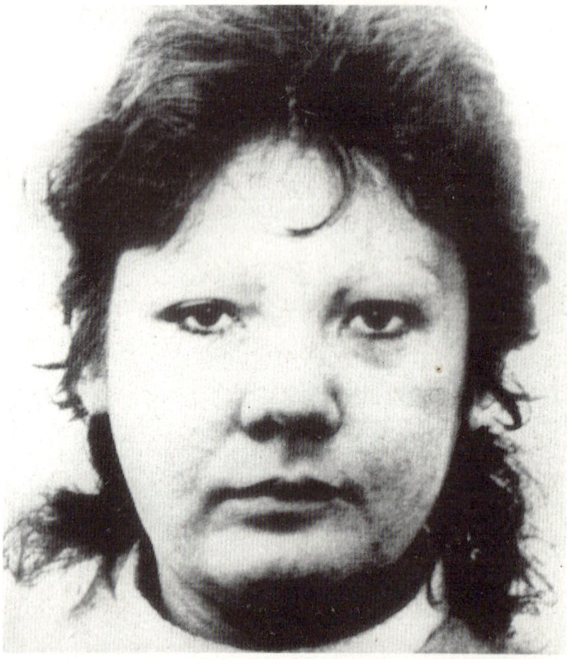

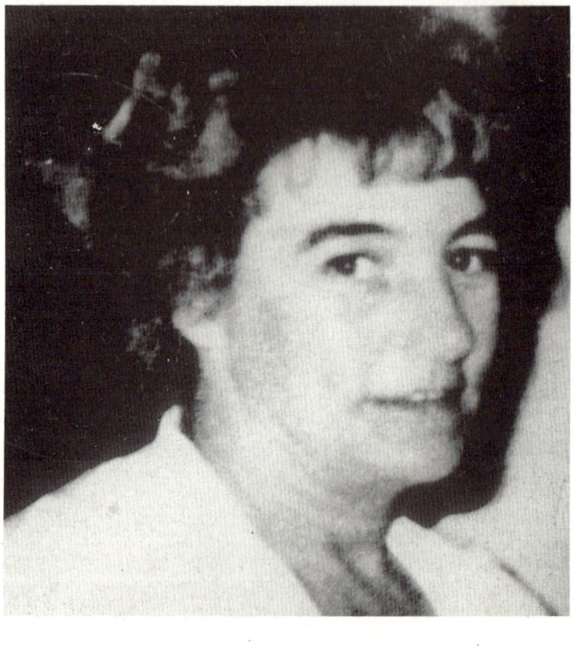

body of Wilma McCann, a 28-year-old prostitute and mother of four children. Her body was found on 30 October 1975, but there had been similar attacks on Yorkshire women before – in July and August of that year. Both the previous victims had been slashed with a knife, but both had survived after brain surgery.

The police warning was one that the head of the local Leeds CID, Chief Superintendent Dennis Hoban, was repeating forcibly less than three months later, when in January 1976 the body of a second prostitute, 42-year-old Emily Jackson, was found in an alleyway in the Chapeltown district of Leeds, an area where prostitution and vice flourished. Her body, too, had been attacked in a frenzy, apparently the work of a psychopath. This was now a story that the newspapers began to pick up but it had already died down when in February 1977, a third body was found and the nation was reminded of the gruesome events of the previous year.

The latest to die was 28-year-old Irene Richardson, another prostitute. She was killed in Roundhay Park, a middle-class area of Leeds, but close to Chapeltown, her body being discovered by a jogger. The link between the three deaths was obvious: all were prostitutes of the Chapeltown area and all had been struck very forcibly on the head and repeatedly cut and stabbed.

The next murder took place less than three months later in Bradford, the nearest city to Leeds. This time the victim, Tina Atkinson, aged 32, was found in her bed, but she, too, was a prostitute and had suffered the same head injuries as the others. Her flat was in Bradford's Lumb Lane area, the equivalent of Leeds' Chapeltown.

Two months later, on 26 June 1977, the British public really woke up to the sequence of horrors that was being inflicted upon the people of Leeds. The fifth murder victim of 'the Ripper' was a pretty 16-year-old, Jayne MacDonald, a happy, energetic girl with lovely blond hair and a striking smile. She was on her way home from a date and crossing a children's playground in Chapeltown when she was struck down

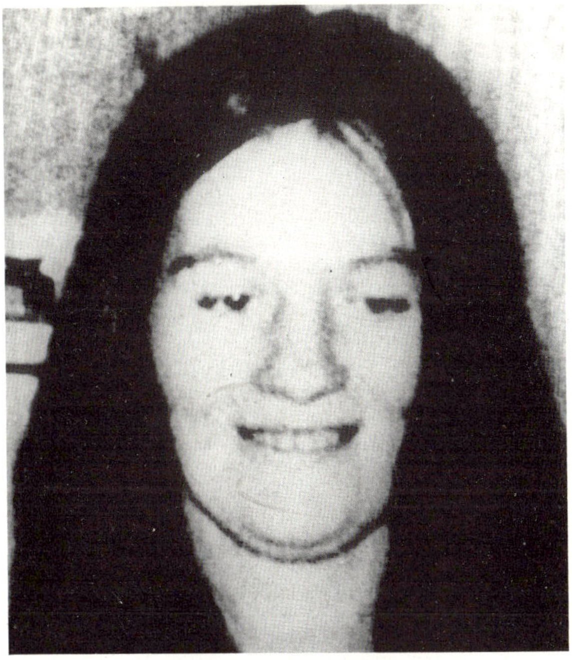

and stabbed like the others. Perhaps the Ripper mistook Jayne MacDonald for a prostitute. From then on a previously indifferent public was alert and anxious to supply the police with any information it could.

Among the next batch of Ripper victims was an innocent teenager, Jayne MacDonald (*bottom left*), whose murder aroused public concern.

A month later 'the Ripper' knocked unconscious a woman he had propositioned in Bradford, but was disturbed when dragging her from the street. She, like earlier victims, recovered after a brain operation. The killer waited just over two months and then moved across the Pennines to Manchester to find his next victim, Jean Jordan, 21, who was battered to death, stabbed repeatedly and left on allotments near a cemetery. When the body was not discovered immediately, he returned eight days later and mutilated it still further, slashing it open from shoulder to legs and attempting to remove the head with a saw. The discovery of the body three days afterwards provided the best clue yet – there was a new £5 note in her handbag. Police were quickly able to trace that it had been issued by the Midland Bank at Shipley, near Bradford, only a few days before. All men employed by companies who drew money from that branch for their wage packets were interviewed by police – and, in fact, as it became known later, 'the Ripper' was among them, but he remained calm and escaped suspicion.

On 31 January 1978 Helen Rytka, 18,

who had just taken up prostitution with her twin sister, was found murdered in a timber yard beneath a railway viaduct in Huddersfield, another West Yorkshire town. In March the body of Yvonne Pearson, 22, prostitute, was found on waste ground in Bradford, one arm protruding from beneath a dumped sofa. She had actually been murdered in January, before Helen Rytka, and her badly battered body had already considerably decomposed. Around this time Dennis Hoban, the police chief who had started the enquiry, died suddenly. Assistant Chief Constable George Oldfield had already taken over the case, and he was to suffer a heart attack in 1979, brought on by overwork in his efforts to catch 'the Ripper'.

On 17 May 1978 Vera Millward, a 41-year-old prostitute, met her death at the hands of 'the Ripper' in the grounds of Manchester's Royal Infirmary. There was a break then, until 4 April 1979,when the Ripper's tenth victim and his second 'innocent' one, Josephine Whitaker, was murdered. A 19-year-old building society clerk, she was taking a short cut home through Savile Park, Halifax, another Yorkshire town, when 'the Ripper' caught up with her. Again, the skull was shattered and the body stabbed repeatedly with a sharpened screwdriver.

By now the cassette mentioned earlier had been sent to Oldfield, and he played the tape at a press conference. Parts of its sensational message ran as follows:

'... the only time (your boys) came near catching me was a few months back in Chapeltown when I was disturbed. Even then it was a uniform copper, not a detective.

I warned you in March that I'd strike again. Sorry it wasn't Bradford. I did promise you that, but I couldn't get there. I'm not quite sure when I will strike again, but it will be definitely sometime this year, maybe September or October, even sooner if I get the chance. I'm not sure where, maybe Manchester. I like it there, there's plenty of them knocking about....'

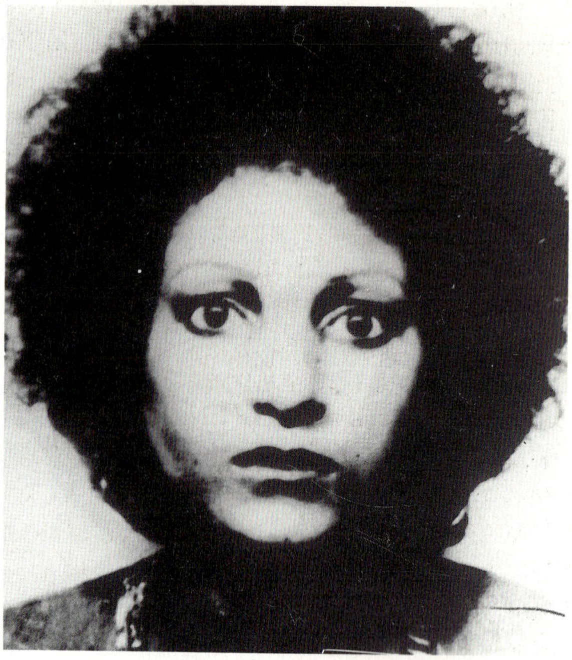

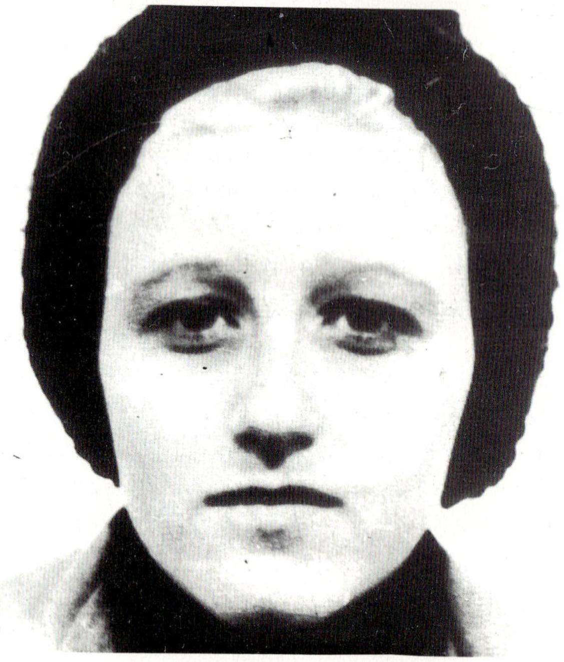

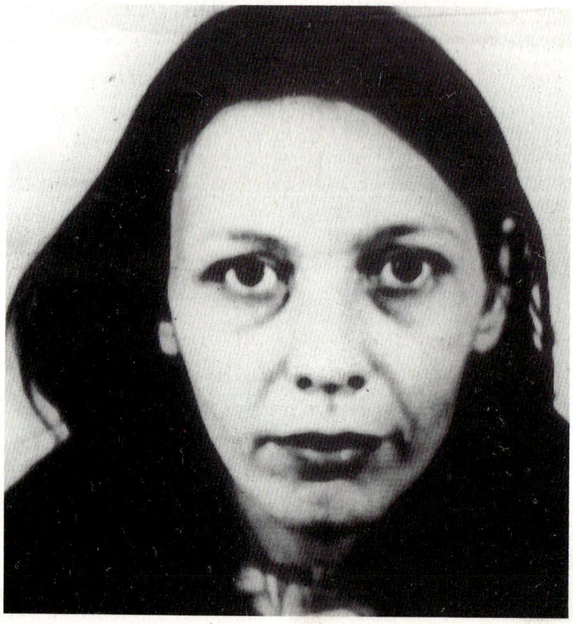

Right
The grim catalogue of deaths continued with the slaying of three more prostitutes.

Barbara Leach, a 20-year-old student at Bradford University, was murdered in the small hours of 2 September 1979 – the Ripper's third victim who was not a prostitute. She was on her way home from meeting friends, and her battered and stabbed body was found in an alleyway, covered with an old carpet held down with bricks.

George Oldfield was confident that the cassette would prove to be 'the Ripper's' mistake. It was closely studied by experts in dialect, and the strong Geordie accent narrowed it down to the Castletown district of Sunderland. From then on everybody believed the Ripper was a Geordie. . . .

The 12th murder victim was another respectable woman, Margo Wells, 47, a civil servant. She was walking home in Pudsey, near Leeds, when she was attacked and strangled with a rope. Her assailant, whom the police at first doubted was 'the Ripper', because of the new manner of killing, stripped her and hid the body beneath grass cuttings in a nearby driveway.

The next two Ripper victims escaped death. A doctor from Singapore was attacked by having a rope thrown round her neck. She was hit on the head, but 'the Ripper', curiously enough, changed his mind when dragging her off the road and fled. On 5 November 1979 – Guy Fawkes night – he knocked to the ground a 16-year-old girl in Huddersfield, but her boyfriend heard her scream and 'the Ripper' ran away at his approach. This narrow escape probably impressed some caution on the murderer, because just over a year passed before he struck again.

The 13th victim, Jacqueline Hill, was a 20-year-old Leeds University student. On 17 November 1980 she was walking home in the evening from the local bus stop when she was struck on the head, dragged behind some bushes, undressed and mutilated with a screwdriver.

The fact that another young and innocent girl had been struck down at only 9.30 in the evening in the middle of staid and respectable Headingley caused a public outcry. The Ripper squad was reorganized

Josephine Whitaker was a building society clerk.

under the command of acting Assistant Chief Constable Jim Hobson of Leeds CID. He began another assessment of all the computerized information held at headquarters and decided to forget the voice on the tape.

However, it was routine police enquiries which eventually led to the capture of 'the Ripper'. This took place in Sheffield, another of the great Yorkshire cities. A prostitute, Ada Rievers, was invited into a Rover, parked in an office driveway, and given £10 by a man, who was, however, unable to have sexual intercourse. The two were sitting in the front seat when a police car arrived to check on the parked cars – the street was known for its use by prostitutes. The man, who gave his name as Peter Williams, was asked to sit in the back of his car while one officer rang through to check the number plates. They were found to be false. He and the girl were taken to the police station, but not before he had been given permission to leave the car in order to urinate against a nearby storage tank. At the police station, he made a second request to go to the lavatory, and was allowed to do so. Later he explained away a rope he was carrying in his pocket, but suddenly the fact that he had relieved himself on two occasions struck a sergeant as suspicious. The storage tank was revisited and a hammer and knife were found, and in the police station cistern

another knife was discovered. Confronted with this, the man confessed he was 'the Ripper'.

The stories which emerged now that Peter William Sutcliffe, the Yorkshire Ripper, had been caught, were embarrassing for the police. It seemed that they had interviewed him at least six times in their enquiries over the years, and some of his workmates had even called him 'the Ripper' in jest because of it.

The cab of his lorry at his workplace, T. and W.H. Clark, an engineering and haulage firm at Shipley, Yorkshire, where he had been interviewed, carried a notice written by himself: 'In this truck is a man whose latent genius, if unleashed, would rock the nation, whose dynamic energy would overpower those around him. Better let him sleep.' If police officers noticed it, they did not consider that its strangeness merited a closer check on its author.

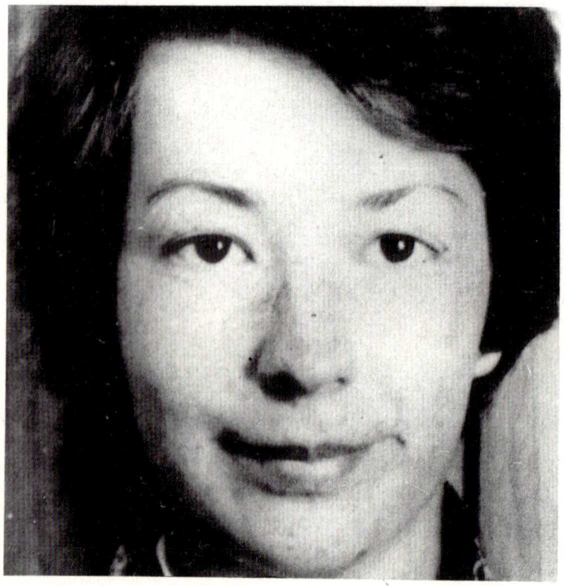

Barbara Leach (*above*) and Jacqueline Hill (*below*) were both university students, and their murders led to calls for immediate action.

Sutcliffe had been born on 2 June 1946, the eldest of five children. A moderate school record did not lead to any good job opportunities, and he held many menial positions, including one as a grave-digger. His defence at his trial was based on insanity, and he claimed that a voice had spoken to him from a cross in the cemetery, instructing him to kill prostitutes. In truth, he probably developed a morbid liking for interfering with corpses while at work.

At the age of 21 he met and began courting a Czech girl, pretty Sonia Szurma, and they married in Bradford on 10 August 1974, her 24th birthday. They were an odd couple: she so demure and shy, yet apparently the dominant personality in their numerous noisy rows, he with a fascination for red light districts – those of Leeds and Bradford in particular.

Sutcliffe's attacks on prostitutes began before his marriage – he said the first was in 1969. He admitted to remorse at his first murder of a girl who was not a prostitute, but claimed that later he was driven to kill any woman.

Sutcliffe was charged with 13 murders and seven attempted murders. At his trial in May 1981 he was found guilty on all counts. He was sentenced to life imprisonment, with a recommendation that he serve at least 30 years.

Sutcliffe's voice, with its Yorkshire accent, is nothing like that of the Geordie on the famous tape recording. That seems to have been a hoax which cruelly misdirected the police and cost hours of wasted time – and perhaps some lives. The hoaxer has not been discovered.

Sutcliffe's wife refused to move from their house, despite the hate campaigns directed against her. In 1989 she was in the headlines again when awarded £600,000 in libel damages against the satirical magazine *Private Eye*, which had suggested, without foundation according to the court, that she had tried to make money from her husband's crimes. This exceptional award was later set aside on appeal.

Lindy Chamberlain and her husband, Michael, leaving the court in Alice Springs.

WHAT HAPPENED TO AZARIA?

An Australian tragedy featuring Ayers Rock and a dingo led to heartbreak for a misunderstood mother.

Maybe the only crime committed at Ayers Rock in August 1980 was by a dog, but it led to one of the most famous legal battles in Australia.

Lindy Chamberlain was accused of murdering her nine-week-old daughter, Azaria. The case attracted attention because Mrs Chamberlain claimed that the baby had been taken by a dingo – an Australian wild dog. It was one of those

A view of Ayers Rock, a remarkable natural formation, visible for many miles around.

issues on which all Australians had an opinion – which could almost be reduced to the question of who was considered the more sympathetic character, the mother or the dog. Normally, of course, in these circumstances a mother would receive nothing but sympathy. But Lindy Chamberlain had a disadvantage – she was a Seventh Day Adventist. This meant, to many of her countryfolk, that she was a crank, for they soon learned, if they didn't know before, that Seventh Day Adventists do not drink anything stimulating and frown upon modern entertainments like the cinema and fripperies like make-up. Moreover, Lindy seemed remarkably cool about the tragedy. And would – could – a dingo really take a baby?

The whole thing started at 8 pm on 17 August 1980. The location was the famous landmark Ayers Rock, in Australia's Northern Territory. As usual a number of holiday makers and trippers were camping below it, including Lindy Chamberlain

and her husband Michael. The 36-year-old Michael was a minister of the Seventh Day Adventist Church. His wife was four years younger, and with them were their three children, Aidan, seven, Reagan, four, and Azaria, who had been born only nine weeks before.

According to Lindy, she was preparing supper outside, the three children having already been put to bed in their tent, when Aidan, who was the only one awake, declared that he was hungry. Lindy brought him outside in order to give him something to eat, leaving the tent flap unzipped, as they would not require more than a few minutes.

However, her husband thought he heard the baby crying, so Lindy made her way back, only to see in the darkness as she neared the tent a dingo walking away from her and apparently shaking its head. When she got to the tent, she found the carrycot empty and the blankets dishevelled. She screamed out that a dingo had taken the

Right
In 1987 Lindy Chamberlain was pardoned after an official enquiry.

baby. Within seconds her husband was on the scene and within minutes many helpers were searching the surrounding land with torches. The local police were sent for, but in the dark, on that awkward rocky terrain, with its bushes and scrub and small trees, they were unable to find anything. In the morning a more organized search was carried out, and the police shot many dingos, hoping to find evidence that one had taken the baby. But the baby and the guilty dingo had vanished.

Naturally, the event was a big news story, and not only in Australia. It was not long before people were remarking on the self-possession of the Chamberlains, and the unfortunate parents became aware that strong suspicions were building up against them. These were not lessened when, eight days after the disappearance of Azaria, some of her clothing was found. It was bloodstained and, oddly enough, her singlet was inside out. Clearly, even if a dingo could have torn the clothes off the baby, could it have done it in such a way that the singlet would be turned inside out? In fact the police were suspicious, even to the extent of putting clothes on a dead goat and feeding it to dingos at Adelaide zoo to see what happened.

The results of this and other tests seemed to cast doubts on the presumption that a dingo was involved, and the inquest was looked forward to with interest. But the verdict in February 1981, in an inquest which was televised because of the immense public interest, was that the baby met her death when taken by a dingo, and some of the more fanciful public rumours about 'religious sacrifices' were exploded.

However, in December of that year, in the light of further police investigations, a new inquest was begun. A policeman told of bloodstains found under the front seat of the Chamberlain's car, only apparent when he unbolted the seats. Michael Chamberlain agreed that he had once cleaned a little blood out of the car – in fact he had given a lift to a man injured in a road accident, and the man came forward to testify. It was suggested that Lindy had sent the tracksuit she had worn on the fatal night to the cleaners and that there had been blood on it. Forensic tests on the baby's clothes indicated that holes had been made by a sharp implement, not teeth, and it was suggested that a pair of bloodstained nail scissors could have been that implement. A British expert, Professor James Cameron, stated that tests on the stretchsuit using ultraviolet light revealed a bloodstained handprint of a woman's size, and that the blood had flowed from above (the implication being that the baby was upright when the blood flowed – possibly from the throat).

All this evidence led to Lindy Chamberlain's being charged with murder, and her husband as an accessory. The seven-week trial, which began on 13 September 1982, was largely a contest between scientific experts, the defence providing those who claimed that the holes in the stretchsuit were made by an animal's teeth and that there was no evidence of a handprint on it.

Mr and Mrs Chamberlain were found guilty. Lindy Chamberlain was sentenced to hard labour for life and Michael to 18 months imprisonment, suspended so that he could look after the other children. Lindy gave birth to another daughter soon after entering prison.

Now that Lindy Chamberlain had been found guilty, those who supported her or sympathized with her commanded more attention. In 1984, after her appeal had

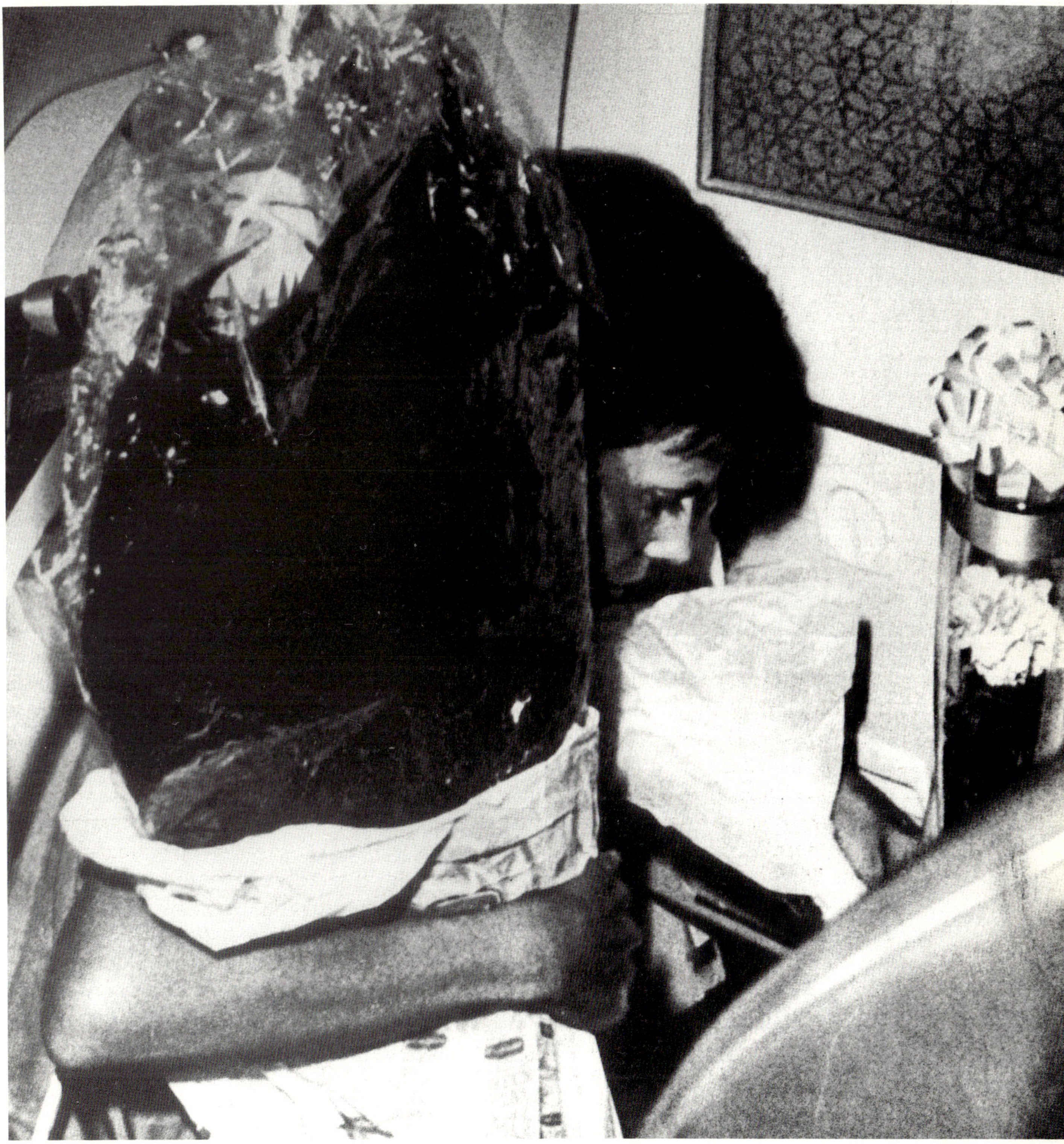

Lindy Chamberlain carrying a bunch of flowers on her release from jail.

been rejected by the high court, another family described how, just before Azaria's disappearance, a dingo had dragged their child from a car at Ayers Rock, and the chief ranger there gave his opinion that dingoes would attack a child.

On 7 February 1986 Lindy was released after just over two years in prison, and began a campaign to establish her innocence. An impressive television interview won many over to her side, including a juror at her trial, who now declared she had changed her mind about Lindy's guilt.

Lindy received so much support that another enquiry was held, headed by Mr Justice Morling, whose conclusion was that the possibility of the child having been taken by a dingo could not be ruled out. Lindy Chamberlain was later pardoned, but promised to continue her fight in order to clear completely the names of herself and her husband.

INDEX

Numbers in italics refer to illustrations

Photographic Acknowledgements

Australian Overseas Information Service, London/D. McNaughton 186–7; The Bettmann Archive, New York 70; The Bettmann Archive, New York/Hulton Deutsch Collection, London 40, 52–3; Camera Press, London 104–5, 108 bottom, 108–9; Camera Press, London/Ray Hamilton 156 (all four); Camera Press, London/Andrew Varley 7 bottom right; The Christchurch Star 110, 111, 112 top and bottom; Mary Evans Picture Library, London 7 top, 18, 19, 20, 20–1, 21; Herald-Sun, Herald & Weekly Times Ltd, Melbourne 75, 76–7; The Hulton-Deutsch Collection, London 4, 10, 12, 29, 30 bottom, 42, 45, 46–7, 56 top and bottom, 58 right, 59, 81, 82–3, 90, 90–1, 91, 148, 152, 155, 161, 172–3; Illustrated London News Picture Library, London 88–9; Kobal Collection, London 32–3, 35; Popperfoto, London 1, 2–3, 7 centre left and centre right, 12–13, 16 left, 23 left, 24, 25 left and right, 31, 41 top left and bottom, 43 bottom, 44, 47, 48, 60–1, 62–3, 63, 64, 65 bottom, 79, 80, 80–1, 83, 84, 85, 86–7, 92–3, 94–5, 95, 96, 97 top and bottom, 98, 99 bottom, 101, 102–3, 106 bottom, 107 bottom right, 114, 116 right, 130 left, 131 bottom, 132, 133 bottom right, 134 top and centre, 136–7, 137 bottom left and bottom right, 138 bottom, 146–7, 150, 153, 154–5, 158–9, 163, 170, 171, 180 (all three), 181 (all four), 182 (all three), 183, 184 top and bottom, 185, 188, 189; Press Association, London 178–9; Reuters/Bettmann Newsphotos 164; Syndication International, London 8–9, 14, 15 top and bottom, 16 right, 16–17, 23 right, 28–9, 30 top, 41 top right, 43 top, 68, 69, 78, 92, 99 top, 100 left and right, 106 top, 107 top and bottom left, 108 top, 113, 115, 116 left, 124–5, 125, 126, 126–7, 127, 128–9, 130 right, 131 top left and top right, 133 top left, top right and bottom left, 134 bottom, 135 top and bottom, 138 top, 139, 160, 162 top and bottom; Ullstein Bilderdienst, Berlin 54 left and right, 55 left and right, 57, 58 left; UPI/Bettmann Newsphotos, New York 7 bottom left, 11, 13, 26–7, 33, 34, 34–5, 36, 37 top and bottom, 38–9, 39, 49, 50, 50–1, 51, 65 top, 66 left and right, 67, 68–9, 71, 72, 72–3, 74, 117, 118–19, 120, 121, 122–3, 140–1, 142–3, 143 bottom, 144, 144–5, 149, 151, 157, 164–5, 166 top and bottom, 167, 168–9, 174, 175, 176–7.